Theos – clear thinking on religion

Theos is the UK's leading religion and society think tank. With over a combined circulation of 160 million in the past 5 years, we are about the role of faith in contemporary society by means of high We provide a credible, informed and gracious Christian voice in our mainstream public conversations.

The *Economist* calls us "an organisation that demands attention", and Julian Baggini, the influential atheist philosopher, has said "Theos provides rare proof that theology can be interesting and relevant even – perhaps especially – for those who do not believe."

To learn more, check us out on social media:

twitter.com/theosthinktank | facebook.com/theosthinktank | www.theosthinktank.co.uk

Why we exist

Religion has emerged as one of the key public issues of the 21st century, both nationally and globally. Our increasingly religiously-diverse society demands that we grapple with religion as a significant force in public life. Unfortunately, much of the debate about the role and place of religion has been unnecessarily emotive and ill-informed. We exist to change that.

We reject the notion of any possible 'neutral' perspective on these issues. We also reject the idea that religion is a purely private matter or that it is possible to divide public and private values for anyone.

We seek, rather, to recognise and analyse the ethical ideas and commitments that underlie public life and to engage in open and honest public debate, bringing the tradition of Christian social and political thought to bear on current issues. We believe that the mainstream Christian tradition has much to offer for a flourishing society.

What we do

Theos conducts research, publishes reports, and holds debates, seminars and lectures on the intersection of religion, politics and society in the contemporary world. We also provide regular comment for print and broadcast media and briefing and analysis to parliamentarians and policy makers. To date, Theos has produced over 50 research reports focusing on the big issues impacting British society, including welfare (*The Future of Welfare: A Theos Collection*), law (*"Speaking Up" – Defending and Delivering Access to Justice Today*), economics (*Just Money: How Catholic Social Teaching can Redeem Capitalism*), multiculturalism (*Making Multiculturalism Work*) and voting reform (*Counting on Reform*), as well as on a range of other religious, legal, political and social issues.

In addition to our independently-driven work, Theos provides research, analysis and advice to individuals and organisations across the private, public and not-for-profit sectors. Our staff and consultants have strong public affairs experience, an excellent research track record and a high level of theological literacy. We are practised in research, analysis, debate, and media relations.

Where we sit

We are committed to the traditional creeds of the Christian faith and draw on social and political thought from a wide range of theological traditions. We also work with many non-Christian and non-religious individuals and organisations.

Theos was launched with the support of the Archbishop of Canterbury and the Cardinal Archbishop of Westminster, but it is independent of any particular denomination. We are an ecumenical Christian organisation, committed to the belief that religion in general and Christianity in particular has much to offer for the common good of society as a whole. We are not aligned with any point on the party political spectrum, believing that Christian social and political thought cuts across these distinctions.

Join the discussion by becoming a Friend of Theos

Impact how society views Christianity and shape the cultural debate

The Friends' Programme is designed specifically for people who wish to enter the heart of the current debate. When you join, our commitment is to keep you informed, equipped, encouraged and inspired so that you can be a voice in the public square with us.

As a member of the Friends' Programme, you are provided with:

- *Hard copies of all our latest reports* on the most pressing issues – social justice, welfare, politics, spirituality, education, money, atheism, humanism…
- *Free access to our events.* Theos hosts a number of high calibre speakers (e.g. Rowan Williams, Larry Siedentop, Grace Davie) and debates ('Magna Carta and the future of liberty', 'Does humanism need Christianity?'). As a friend, you will receive invitations to all these without charge.
- *A network of like-minded people* who wish to share ideas and collaborate with one another. We host networking events which help you meet fellow Friends and build your own network, allowing ideas to flow and connections to form.
- *Our monthly e-newsletter* which is your one-stop digest for the latest news regarding religion and society.
- **If you join as an Associate**, you are *invited to private functions with the team*, allowing you to discuss upcoming projects, review the latest issues and trends in society, and have your say in where you see the public debate is going.

You can become a Friend or Associate today by visiting our website
www.theosthinktank.co.uk

If you'd prefer additional information, you can write to us directly:
Friends Programme, Theos, 77 Great Peter Street, London, SW1P 2EZ

If you have any inquiries regarding the Programme, you can email us at:
friends@theosthinktank.co.uk

A soul for the union

Ben Ryan

acknowledgements

Sections of this report draw extensively on research carried out by the author for an MSc Dissertation at the European Institute of the London School of Economics and thanks are due to the staff at that department for their help and advice for that work.

The author is extremely grateful for the support of the Christian Political Foundation for Europe (CPFE), for their generous contribution towards this project, and to various colleagues and friends at Theos and elsewhere who have read drafts and given their advice. Special thanks are due to Professor John Loughlin for providing the foreword.

Published by Theos in 2015
© Theos

ISBN 978-0-9931969-2-8

Some rights reserved – see copyright licence for details
For further information and subscription details please contact:

Theos
Licence Department
77 Great Peter Street
London
SW1P 2EZ

T 020 7828 7777
E hello@theosthinktank.co.uk
www.theosthinktank.co.uk

contents

foreword — 6

introduction — 8

chapter 1: the early dream — 13

chapter 2: Europe today — 21

chapter 3: putting a soul (back) in the union — 37

foreword

British citizens will soon be confronted with a referendum that will ask them whether they wish to remain members of the European Union or leave it – the inelegantly named 'Brexit' option. We need to have a mature debate about this and Ben Ryan of Theos has done us a great service in this report by recalling dimensions of the issue that tend to be ignored: the moral and, indeed, religious aspects of the debate.

Ryan usefully places the European project in its historical context. It was originally a response by some European political leaders, mainly but not exclusively Catholic Christian Democrats, to the catastrophe of the Second World War and, indeed, to the several armed conflicts that had pitted the nations of Europe against each other since the 19th century. Furthermore, during the Second World War, the ideology of Nazism had, in a crazy and irrational orgy of violence, attempted to exterminate entire groups of people as well as reducing whole cities to rubble. The EU's founding fathers saw Nazism and Fascism as outgrowths of nationalism and sought to devise a system which, while not denying the existence of nation-states, would ensure they were contained.

It was the moral vision of the dignity of every human person that underlay the European project. The Theos report, however, accurately describes the slow attenuation of this moral vision over the fifty years of the European Union's existence. As early as the 1950s, the economic and financial aspects – from a common market to a single currency – began to predominate over the political and moral vision of the founders. The institutions became largely impersonal bureaucracies regulating the functioning of the market. Furthermore, the EU has been largely elite-driven and has slowly lost touch with the peoples of Europe. These developments are unfortunate as they obscure the very real achievements of the Union and, not least, the fact that there has been no major war between European states since 1945. The European Union was a key factor in the successful transition to democracy of the former communist states of East and Central Europe. Even peace in the Balkans has been at least partly due to the *prospect* of EU membership. Finally, there exists today a much greater closeness among European peoples, especially the young, thanks to various schemes such as the Erasmus student exchange programme and ease of travel across borders.

Despite these accomplishments, it is clear, as Ryan argues in this report, that in the actual functioning of the EU, there are also problems, many of which derive from the failure of moral vision of *today's* elites. He does not advocate a return to the past, which is in any case impossible, but a reformulation of a moral vision to meet contemporary challenges such as the democratic deficit, the aberrant dominance of market-based approaches to public policy, the migrant and refugee crisis, and the environment. Furthermore, as Popes John Paul II and Benedict XVI continually reiterated, Europe should not turn its back on its Christian roots which have shaped its values and institutions. This does not mean a return to Christendom but a return to a deeper and wider understanding of what it means to be a European.

Professor John Loughlin,
Blackfriars, Oxford and Emeritus Fellow, St Edmund's College, Cambridge

introduction

the UK and Europe – why the debate matters

At some point in 2016 voters in the UK will take part in what could be one of the defining moments of 21st century history – both in Europe and the wider world. Should they vote to leave the European Union it will be a seismic shock for the dream of European unity and might signal the beginning of the end for what has been the most ambitious and innovative international political project in modern history.

The European Union is a unique experiment, one sufficiently unusual that it has demanded the invention of new social science terminology in order to define it adequately. There have been other political unions before (such as the United Kingdom itself), other economic areas or custom unions (such as NAFTA, the North Atlantic Free Trade Area, or Benelux), and there have been other multilateral international organizations (such as the UN, Nordic Council, and NATO). And, of course, there have been states that have engulfed different nations and regions and brought them under a single, imperial rule. There has never been, however, such an ambitious effort to pool sovereignty, synchronise regulation, and remove internal barriers and borders as the EU has established in modern times.

Since the Treaty of Paris that established the European Coal and Steel Community (ECSC) in 1951 among the 'original six' (Belgium, Netherlands, France, Luxembourg, Italy, and West Germany), the European project has grown enormously. A succession of treaties has seen new members and expansions of the capacity and ambition of the project. In 2013, Croatia became the 28th member of the European Union, and there are five states (Iceland, the Former Yugoslav Republic of Macedonia, Montenegro, Serbia, and Turkey) that are currently in negotiations as officially recognised applicant candidates.

As a 20th century project, 'Europe' was remarkably successful. When the EU won the Nobel Peace Prize in 2012 it was met with some mockery,[1] yet the successful reconciliation of West Germany and France should not be too easily dismissed. It was the post-war foreign policy priority highest prized by both the USA and Winston Churchill, and one they saw as among the most difficult to accomplish (above even, at least initially, the threat of the

USSR to Europe). In May 1950, having seen proposals for the ECSC, John Foster Dulles, the then US Acting Secretary of State (later Secretary of State under Eisenhower) said:

> While obviously many details are lacking necessary for final judgement, it is my initial impression that the conception is brilliantly creative and could go far to solve the most dangerous problem of our time, namely the relationship of Germany's industrial power to France and the West.[2]

Sixty-five years later, after decades of growth and a remarkable expansion that now includes much of what once lay behind the Iron Curtain, the European Union for the first time looks in real danger of losing members. In Greece, the EU faces a particular issue, in which economic austerity and populist government have combined to create an impasse that might yet force an exit. The character of the UK's potential exit, however, is arguably far more damaging. Greece is not, even now, fundamentally anti-European. Indeed, it is the Greek people's over-riding desire to see their nation remain within the Euro that has been essential to it doing so. Moreover, Greece is a relatively small economy and not an especially powerful member state, even regionally in the Balkans.

The UK, by contrast, will not leave because it has been backed into a corner by imposed austerity. It is the second biggest economy in the EU (behind only Germany, having overtaken France in 2015).[3] It remains a significant international power, with a seat on the UN Permanent Security Council, prominent status in NATO, nuclear capability, and, in the Commonwealth, one of the most significant soft-power international leadership roles in the world. Greece leaving the EU would be a disconcerting bump for a European project which has never previously shrunk. The loss of the UK would be a far more severe blow in terms of economic power and global diplomatic prestige.

The stakes for Europe are, therefore, high. They are also significant for the very model of global governance that Europe exemplifies. A 'Brexit' would probably not signal the end of the continued expansion of the EU, either to new countries or the ever closer union that may well now be inevitable at least in the Eurozone. But it would be a significant blow to any hope of turning this model into the norm for global governance. A union that is perceived as no longer having a benefit for powerful nations is one which is unlikely to gain appeal in other regions of the world.

> *A union that is perceived as no longer having a benefit for powerful nations is one which is unlikely to gain appeal in other regions of the world.*

the stagnation of the debate

The Europe debate in the UK has been at the forefront of politics for some years now, with the rise of UKIP and the strength of the Eurosceptic wing of the Conservative party well-documented. With prominence, unfortunately, has not come a corresponding quality of argument or information. Too many myths, scaremongering stories and half-truths dominate the rhetoric of both sides. Perhaps most depressing, however, is the fact that the entire debate on both sides has become reduced to a contest between economic calculations without space for the earlier concerns concerning the moral and social aspects of the European project.

Take, for example, an article which appeared on the BBC website in May 2013.[4] In its own words, it is "a summary of the key arguments for and against British membership". Most of the article is then taken up with debates on taxation, costs, trade, and jobs. Only two points really deal with anything else, namely global influence and sovereignty. This is symptomatic of a broader trend in which the debate has been reduced to technical speculation and massaging of figures to demonstrate which option provides the better financial outlook.

This is replicated across the EU. The rhetoric everywhere is about financial growth and security at all costs. In the response to the Eurocrisis, welfare funding has been slashed. Greek pensions have been brutally cut, with the *Guardian* reporting that nearly 45 per cent of Greece's 2.5 million retirees now live on incomes of less than €665 a month – below the poverty line defined by the EU.[5] Youth unemployment is around 50 per cent in Greece and Spain, and astonishingly high in Italy and Portugal as investment has been cut back.[6] Rhetoric over solidarity and maintaining peace and prosperity for the people has transformed into a Union-wide obsession with cutting deficits and shrinking the state. Protecting the Euro and reducing the deficit have become a far greater concern than protecting vulnerable people or supporting employment.

Debate across the continent is on how to achieve these economic targets at the expense of all else. Somehow and somewhere along the line, the sense of what Europe was for and why it mattered has changed. The vision of the founding fathers of Europe – Alcide De Gasperi, Konrad Adenauer, Robert Schuman, Jean Monnet, Paul-Henri Spaak, and even Churchill – is unrecognisable in the debates over Europe today. What was once a project based on morality, peace, and the prosperity and advantage of Europe's people has become something quite different.

This essay traces that conception of the basis of Europe. In the first part it argues that the early European project had a profound sense of its own identity, one that was fundamentally *moral* and based on the principle of *solidarity*. It was, at least then, a conception which was intimately tied up with a vision drawn from Christian, and particularly Catholic political and social theory.

That vision seems to have faded (although it is still there in parts and perhaps can yet be revived), and the second part of this essay will look at our contemporary Europe, the rise of technocratic economics and the weakness of an identity based on anything as fickle as economic performance.

> *What was once a project based on morality, peace, and the prosperity and advantage of Europe's people has become something quite different.*

The third and final part will point towards a stronger vision for a Europe worth defending. Regardless of the way the UK chooses to vote in its referendum, there is a problem for Europe. If it makes its claim and stakes its identity on market 'fundamentalism' and the vagaries of economic performance it will never be able to inspire genuine solidarity and promote a real European identity and *demos*. Authentic political affection and identity is based on deeper bonds than the promise of a slightly improved national economy. A Europe worth defending needs to discover, or rediscover, its soul.

introduction – references

1. The *Economist* editorial by Charlemagne was simply entitled 'Hmmm', while the *New Statesman* more explicitly argued 'Why the EU doesn't deserve the Nobel Peace Prize'.
2. Letter to the US Secretary of State, 10 May 1950.
3. Reported by the Centre for Economics and Business Research and others - http://www.cebr.com/reports/world-economic-league-table-2015/
4. 'UK and the EU: Better off out or in?' http://www.bbc.co.uk/news/uk-politics-20448450
5. 'Fight to save the Greek pension takes centre stage in Brussels and Athens' *The Guardian*, 21 May 2015.
6. *Trading Economics* records May 2015 data that has Greece, youth unemployment at 49.70 per cent, Spain's at 49.30 per cent, Italy's at 41.50 per cent, Portugal's at 33.30 per cent, Croatia's at 43.60 per cent and Cyprus' at 34.40 per cent – http://www.tradingeconomics.com/european-union/youth-unemployment-rate (accessed 10 July 2015). Others have cited it even higher, including the *Economist* in May 2015.

the early dream

a (very) brief history of the European project

Following the chaos of the Second World War the first major step on the way to what is now the EU was the 1951 Treaty of Paris that established the ECSC (European Coal and Steel Community) among the 'original six' (West Germany, France, Italy, Luxembourg, Netherlands, and Belgium). In 1958, this was updated by the Treaty of Rome to become the EEC (European Economic Community).

The first expansion of this small club came in 1973 with the accession of the UK, Ireland and Denmark. This was followed by Greece in 1981, and, once they had come out of their respective dictatorships, Spain and Portugal in 1986. The real growth, though, came after the Maastricht Treaty of 1992 that established the European Union and European Monetary Union (EMU). Following that change the EU was joined, in 1995, by Austria, Sweden and Finland and, in 2004, in a giant single accession, by Estonia, Lithuania, Latvia, the Czech Republic, Malta, Cyprus, Hungary, Poland, Slovakia, and Slovenia.

The process of enlargement (to date) was completed by the accession of Bulgaria and Romania in 2007 and Croatia in 2013, with the Lisbon Treaty coming into force in 2009. Each new treaty and accession has changed the character of the European project such that it can be difficult to detect accurately the original priorities and influences. It is a fair question to wonder whether the founding fathers of the European project would recognise the entity of today as anything for which they could have laid the ground work.

the origins of the project

There have been several different models for a unified Europe. Most of these have, historically, taken the form of imperial projects to conquer Europe, with unity realised by military power. In the wake of the Second World War, however, there were a number of proposals and proponents of a more peaceful unity stemming from very different political and philosophical traditions.

The colourfully-named Count Richard Nikolaus von Coudenhove-Kalergi was one such visionary. His father was an Austro-Hungarian diplomat and his mother the Japanese daughter of a major oil merchant and landowner. He was founder and president of the Paneuropa Union – a project aimed at unifying Europe in an "ad-hoc politico-economic federation",[1] a movement which collected a remarkable intellectual celebrity following including Richard Strauss, Albert Einstein and Paul Valéry, and even some political support, from figures including sometime French Prime Minister Aristide Briand (sometime because French politics between 1909, when he was first Prime Minister, and 1932 when he died were volatile in the extreme and Briand gained and lost power several times), and Italian foreign minister Carlo Sforza. However, despite its success in attracting a following in popular intellectual circles, the Paneuropa movement never really gained much momentum in affecting actual political change.

Neither, in practice, despite expectations to the contrary, did the Resistance movements create the networks to allow for serious political unity. There had been hopes that the interactions between different WWII Resistance groups would create meaningful connections that might inspire political dialogue. Without a common enemy, however, the networks proved too disparate, and in particular there was an irreconcilable conflict between the Communist Resistance and their support of the USSR, and the other Resistance groups that were as opposed to the communists as they had been to the Nazis.

The network which did inspire the model of European integration that took off in the 1950s was that of Christian Democrat parties and politicians. One manifestation of this was the role, identified by Wolfram Kaiser, played by the Nouvelles Équipes Internationales (NEI) and Geneva Circle of Christian Democrats.[2] Those networks provided discussion forums and introduced key Catholic political figures to one another. So, for example, French Prime Minister Robert Schuman's[3] proposal for the ECSC came as no surprise to the German Chancellor Konrad Adenauer[4] since it had often been discussed in NEI and Geneva Circle meetings even before the Second World War.[5] Integration can only have been eased by such connections – for example Josef Müller who served as a link between the German CSU and French MRP Christian Democrat parties and met with Pope Pius XII, Italian Prime Minister Alcide De Gasperi[6] and Schuman between 1945 and 1946. These links allowed for a common ideology to form between Catholic politicians who, following the war, found themselves in a position of unprecedented power and with opportunity to express that ideology in new forms of integration.

This position of power cannot be understated. Though other political parties, notably the Socialists, played their part in early European integration it was the Christian Democrats who dominated the politics of the original six members. This can be easily seen by looking at the signatories for the six countries of the first two treaties of European integration

(Paris in 1951 and Rome in 1958). The Treaty of Rome, for example, with the exception of Paul-Henri Spaak[7] and the two French signatories (all Socialists) was signed almost entirely by Catholic members of Christian Democrat parties. Spaak's fellow signatory from Belgium, Baron Jean Charles Snoy et D'Oppeurs was a Catholic politician with expertise in Thomist philosophy. Luxembourg's Joseph Bech was another leading Catholic figure, as was Dutch signatory Joseph Luns. At Paris, both Belgian signatories were Catholics with interest in Catholic social teaching and again the Dutch provided a Catholic signatory. In both treaties Catholic politicians far outnumbered the others. Among the leading figures (De Gasperi, Schuman, Adenauer) so pronounced were their respective commitments to Catholicism that they were nicknamed the 'Black Front'.[8]

It was from this Christian Democrat setting that the ECSC and EEC came through the treaties of Paris and Rome. That was the political context that defined the early European project – six countries dominated by Christian Democratic parties in the afterward of a destructive conflict that had discredited nationalist parties and an emerging Cold War in which socialism was viewed with significant suspicion by many in Western Europe and by the backers of European integration in the USA and UK.

the content of the early dream

The essential content of what characterised the early European project can be summarised in three areas:

1. Solidarity
2. Subsidiarity
3. Explicit moral/religious vision

Each of these three areas has different components within it but together they characterise the essential ideology of the European project in the 1950s.

solidarity

> Europe will not be made all at once or according to a single plan. It will be built through concrete achievements which first create a *de facto* solidarity.

Those words are drawn from the famous "Schuman Declaration" delivered in May 1950. This public declaration by Robert Schuman, then French Foreign Minister, led directly to the negotiations which culminated in the Paris treaty and the establishment of the ECSC.

The explicit aim referred to repeatedly throughout the early integration process was that of solidarity. What that actually means is less obvious but it seems to have a number of elements – one was peace (or solidarity between nations for mutual benefit). A second was solidarity with workers and the poor (i.e. not so much between nations as between classes). Finally, there was a concern to create political harmony by limiting the power of national politicians.

Peace between nations (and particularly France and Germany) was an obvious starting point for European integration. The failure after the Great War to maintain peace for even a generation and the extraordinary scale of not only military but civilian death in the Second World War made peace an absolute priority. What marked out early European integration was the extraordinary commitment that extended beyond treaties to assuring a basis for peace by making militarisation via coal and steel impossible. In Schuman's words, "the solidarity in production thus established will make it plain that any war between France and Germany becomes not only unthinkable but materially impossible,"[9] because the ECSC required a pooling of sovereignty over the two industries necessary for arming a military and prevented Germany from rapidly outstripping the French industrial sector.

This was a remarkable development, one that surprised and delighted the Americans, who had never thought the French would accept any such proposal, never mind propose it. Crucially, the aim was always peace and solidarity; the potential economic gains were a secondary objective. The German chancellor Adenauer made it quite clear in the Bundestag in 1952 that he felt all six governments involved "realise… that the political goal, the political meaning of the European Coal and Steel Community, is infinitely larger than its economic purpose."[10]

> The aim was always peace and solidarity; the potential economic gains were a secondary objective.

Peace was the primary aim of solidarity, but that did not mean prosperity was excluded, and indeed a concern for prosperity was particularly clear in the Treaty of Rome that established the EEC (European Economic Community) in 1958. However, it is notable that this prosperity was conceived differently than it seems to be today. The focus was on making workers and citizens wealthier, healthier and safer whereas today's focus seems to have lost the recognition that economic prosperity only matters if it improves the lives of citizens.

The commitment is explicitly to "the constant improvement of the living and working conditions of their [member states'] peoples."[11] This commitment is referred to extensively in both the Treaty of Rome and of Paris (see, for example, Articles 2-3 of both treaties), and in Article 117 of Rome which states that "Member states agree upon the need to promote improved working conditions and an improved standard of living for workers."

It is something of an irony that the founders of the European project were the architects and greatest supporters of the developing welfare states in their respective countries, when today Europe seems to be one of the threats to the welfare state – whether in the form of immigration seeming to undermine the system in the UK, or in austerity being imposed on Greece and Spain at the expense of parts of the welfare state. Certainly that (admittedly sometimes rather paternalist) commitment to the welfare state was present in the early stages of European integration.

A final constituent element of solidarity is the commitment to political harmony. In contemporary debates over the EU much is made of the "democratic deficit" – that is, the extent to which European institutions fail adequately to demonstrate their democratic accountability. The early European institutions were designed in part precisely to avoid democratic clashes of the Westminster parliamentary style. The Commission was meant to be a-political and based on consensus (there was also no majority voting). This reflects a wider concern among the founders of the European project to prioritise harmony (a term that appears remarkably frequently across the two treaties in question).

On a broader scale, there was a deliberate intention to limit the power and sovereignty of nation states. Following two world wars and, from the perspective of the Catholic Church and Catholic politicians, a long culture war, the temptation to blame the state for the ills of the modern world was high. Indeed, it was the deliberate efforts at curtailing national power and sovereignty (along, interestingly, with a fear of how the unions would respond) that prevented the UK's Labour post-war government from signing the treaties at the time.[12]

subsidiarity

Subsidiarity, according to the glossary of the EU website, is a concept that:

> [E]nsures that decisions are taken as closely as possible to the citizen and that constant checks are made to verify that action at Union level is justified in light of the possibilities available at national, regional or local level. Specifically, it is the principle whereby the Union does not take action (except in the areas that fall within its exclusive competence), unless it is more effective than action taken at national, regional or local level.[13]

Interestingly, despite being at the heart of the European debate since the foundation of the European project, the term only first appeared in a treaty in the Maastricht Treaty of 1992 which established the European Union. The term was adapted from the 1931 Papal Encyclical *Quadragesimo Anno (QA)*.[14] Wolfram Kaiser notes that at least as early as the

Nouvelles Équipes Internationales (NEI) congress in Tours, 1953 (a meeting of Christian Democrat politicians from across Western Europe), the French politician Pierre-Henri Teitgen suggested basing Christian Democratic policy on *Quadragesimo Anno*. It has an explicit grounding, therefore, in Catholic Social Teaching (CST).

Critically not only was this seen as an issue of governance, but one of justice. Indeed, in *QA* Pope Pius XI summarised the concept of subsidiarity in terms of justice:

> It is an injustice and at the same time a grave evil and disturbance of right order to assign to a greater and higher association what lesser and subordinate organisations can do.

This is tied into a broader conception of how society should function. Christian democracy as an ideology emphasised 'personalism', the idea that all people are fundamentally relational and tied to others. Humans are not atomized individuals but are essentially bound into social structures and particularly families. The emphasis on supporting families and local communities while resisting centralised power found in the doctrine of subsidiarity is one that it is critical to the model of Christian democracy and, therefore, the early European project.

moral and religious vision

To say that there was a distinct moral and religious vision can sound more sectarian than perhaps was the reality. So far this part of the essay has argued that the early European project was defined largely by the priorities of Christian Democrats, with a focus on solidarity and subsidiarity that was based on a particular conception of justice and morality. However, it was never intended to be exclusive in its focus. De Gasperi characterised the Christian aspect of the project by saying:

> When I affirm that Christianity is at the origin of the European Civilisation I do not intend to introduce any kind of exclusive confessional criterion into the evaluation of our history. I refer to the common European heritage, to that unitary morality that puts emphasis on the human being and his responsibility.[15]

This, then, was a vision that came out of a particular ideology and religious tradition that emphasised human responsibility, but was not intended to be limited to any one group. The early European project has been called by the academic Scott Thomas "an act of theopolitical imagination."[16] Even in its earliest days, when the key protagonists were overwhelmingly Catholics from Christian Democrat parties there was a broader sense among observers of the necessity of a legitimately moral and spiritual vision.

Winston Churchill, no Christian Democrat, and certainly no Catholic, commented in his famous Zurich speech:

> We must build a United States of Europe. In this way only will hundreds of millions of toilers be able to regain the simple joys and hopes which make life worth living. The process is simple. All that is needed is the resolve of hundreds of millions of men and women to do right instead of wrong and gain as their reward blessing instead of cursing… There can be no revival of Europe without a spiritually great France and a spiritually great Germany.[17]

There was something of a consensus in the 1940s and 50s, even among those countries that did not join the early integration process, that this was a body that, while it might have particular weaknesses (the Americans were concerned about the possible creation of business cartels, the British about a European bloc inimical to their own interests), was certainly a project of *moral* integrity and importance. This sense – of the critical part that morality, spirituality and indeed religiously-inspired-politics – is something that, as the next part of this essay will argue, has significantly waned since the origins of the European Project.

> *"We must build a United States of Europe"*
> *Winston Churchill*

chapter one – references

1. *Paneuropa* – but here from a translated quotation in Derek Heater, *The Idea of European Unity*, (Leicester University Press, 1992).
2. Wolfram Kaiser, *Christian Democracy and the Origins of European Union*, (Cambridge: Cambridge University Press, 2007).
3. Robert Schuman was born in Luxembourg but was twice Prime Minister of France and the leading figure in the short-lived French Christian Democrat party the MRP (Mouvement Républicain Populaire).
4. Konrad Adenauer was the German (and then West German) Chancellor from 1945 to 1967 and founder of the CDU (Christian Democrat Union) party.
5. Kaiser, *Christian Democracy*, p. 224.
6. Alcide De Gasperi founded the Italian Christian Democrat party that was to be in power almost continuously from 1945 to 1994. He was Prime Minister from 1945-53, an unusual longevity for an Italian Prime Minister.
7. One of the great visionaries of the European project among European socialists, he was a three-time Prime Minister of Belgium, a Secretary General of NATO, and a President of the UN General Assembly.
8. Noted by Heater, *European Unity*, p. 153.
9. Schuman declaration, 9 May 1950.
10. From a speech delivered in the Bundestag as Chancellor of the Federal Republic of Germany, 12 July 1952.
11. Preamble to Treaty of Rome.
12. Cabinet minutes, 22 June 1950.
13. From EU website glossary http://europa.eu/legislation_summaries/glossary/subsidiarity_en.htm
14. Kaiser, *Christian Democracy*, p. 229.
15. Quoted in Venneri and Ferrara (2010) 'Alcide de Gasperi and Antonio Messineo: A Spiritual Idea of Politics and a Pragmatic Idea of Religion?' in *Religion, Politics and Law in the European Union* ed. Leustean and Madeley, (Routledge, 2013) p. 118.
16. Scott Thomas, *The Global Resurgence of Religion and the Transformation of International Relations*. (London: Palgrave Macmillan, 2005) p.167.
17. Extract taken from Churchill's speech at Zurich, 19 September 1946.

Europe today

the new context

The world of today is, of course, very different from that of the 1950s and it is no surprise that the institutions and political bodies deemed appropriate then have naturally evolved in the interim period. For the European project some of the ways in which the context in which it finds itself have changed have had a fundamental impact on its character and identity.

One obvious change is the geopolitical situation. The greatest immediate priority in the 1940s and early 1950s was not the USSR but the difficulty in reconciling France and Germany (later West Germany). That this was achieved relatively quickly is no doubt due in part to the early European project, but also the growth in significance of the Cold War and threat from the USSR.

In our own time both of those issues – the prospect of conflict between France and Germany, and the Cold War – are over (albeit Russia is once again becoming a significant military threat on the borders of European Union members). The concern to protect peace in Europe and to be part of a counterbalance to the threat of communism has abated. This shift is evident among European citizens. In 2011, a Eurobarometer poll found that only four per cent of Europeans considered war or civil war to be the most important challenge to national security.[1] By contrast, 33 per cent rated economic and financial crises as the biggest security threat and 25 per cent chose terrorism.

This shifting concern is also evident among political leaders. While the early European project had an explicit focus on peace that was also widely supported by observers such as the American State Department and the British Foreign Office, today the threat of war within Europe is a less significant policy issue. The re-emergence of a militarised and more aggressive Russian state is changing that issue a bit, at least in Eastern Europe and among the Baltic member states, yet it remains a far more secondary concern than it once was.

One way of illustrating this is to analyse which areas of the European project have seen significant advances in integration. There has been significant integration on economic issues (particularly, of course, on issues surrounding the introduction of the common currency) and yet very little on foreign policy matters. The failure of the European community to respond effectively to the Bosnian crisis on its own doorstep led to some interest and growth in desire to see a more cohesive foreign policy, and the Lisbon Treaty established a 'High Representative of the Union for Foreign Affairs and Security Policy'[2] and the European External Action Service (EEAS). Despite this, the relative impotence of the Union to confront significant external threats, and the reluctance of national politicians to do anything to address that is symptomatic of a general lack of urgency on the issue. Peace, quite simply, no longer resonates as a significant European concern today and that immediately changes the focus of what a European Union is meant to achieve.

Beyond the broader geopolitical context, another significant change is the character of society and politics in the member states. A critical shift since the early European project has been the decline of Christian Democracy and the new dimension brought in by the new member states.

> *The decline of Christian Democracy has been dramatic.*

The decline of Christian Democracy has been dramatic. In the 1950s, Christian Democrat parties dominated politics in Belgium, the Netherlands, Luxembourg, West Germany, and Italy and were a small but important element in French politics. Throughout most of the period between 1950 and 1990 they continued to be a huge presence in those national parliaments and more often than not played a part in government.

Among new members (i.e. other than those original six), only Austria had a Christian Democratic party which had been involved in the NEI[3] and Geneva Circle that had been so influential in bringing together the Christian Democrats of the 1940s and 50s. Plenty of the new members had significant Catholic populations, and indeed Catholic political parties, but for one reason or another they represented different political traditions and ideologies. The most significant transition, however, has been in the original six. The French Christian Democrat party (the MRP), always a small, if influential force even in the 1950s, quickly faded into complete obscurity. The Belgian and Dutch parties remained significant but suffered serious electoral defeats throughout the 1990s. The Italian Christian Democrat party having been continuously in power until the 1990s suffered what must rank as one of the most extraordinarily rapid declines in electoral history, collapsing entirely in the 1990s. The EPP (European People's Party – the European parliamentary party that originally represented Christian Democrat parties) still remains the largest bloc in the European Parliament, but that owes more to the presence of conservative parties than to true Christian democrats today. Even allowing for a revival of sorts in the early to mid-2000s, it is undeniable that Christian Democracy is not the force it once was.

The new member states, and particularly those from Central and Eastern Europe that joined from the 2004 enlargement onwards, bring a very different political culture and history to the Europe of today. The legacy of communism remains a serious policy and identity issue in many of these countries.

In the Balkans, the violent break-up of Yugoslavia likewise is very much a live issue – perhaps nowhere more so than in Croatia, where the former General Ante Gotovina, viewed by many as a national hero, is now a prominent political figure whose intervention in the Europe debate was seen by some as critical in Croatia joining the EU.[4] Gotovina, despite huge popularity in Croatia, is a controversial figure in the Balkans, and was tried and initially found guilty in The Hague of "committing war crimes and crimes against humanity, including murder, deportation, persecution and inhuman acts" during the conflict. He was later acquitted on appeal.[5] These issues of identity, memory and victimhood are potent political forces. They are all the more difficult to reconcile and fix through the European project because, unlike the original six after World War Two, it is not a shared experience or trauma across the member states but a succession of very different national traumas and legacies.

All this illustrates how the political and identity context of the European project has changed in a way that should naturally affect how the Union develops and expresses its purpose. There are two particular (and closely related) manifestations of change which demonstrate what has happened in Europe over the past few decades.

The first is that the European economic orthodoxy has changed from a paternalist Christian Democrat model which saw economics as a tool to deliver solidarity and improved standards of living, to a more free market dominated model in which the market and economic performance indicators have become an end in themselves, even at the expense of other stated aims. This trend has become significantly more pronounced in the response of Europe to its economic crisis and is reaching its apex in the difficult negotiations with the debtor countries (especially Greece). A consensus has been allowed to build up that the primary, perhaps exclusive value of Europe lies in national economic interest – i.e. will *we* – the British or Spanish or Slovaks – be 'better off' in or out of Europe? This consensus is ultimately dangerous to the European project as it is fundamentally less sustainable than the old model of what Europe was for.

Second, and closely related, is the decline of the European project's sense of moral and spiritual purpose. What was once a cohesive identity and ideology based on particular moral concerns has been hollowed out and allowed itself to be replaced by the economic consensus. This ultimately weakens the European project and lowers the sights of its ambition. I will examine each of these key issues in turn.

the changing nature of European economic orthodoxy

The economic model promoted in the early European project, as argued above, owed much to Christian Democratic ideology. Often depicted as a "middle way", there was an emphasis on a fairly paternalist model of political economics with support for the welfare state and a concern to raise prosperity and living standards particularly for workers. The development of a free trade area was explicitly intended as part of a programme that was broader than simply economic, as Adenauer made clear in 1952 with his statement that "the political meaning of the European Coal and Steel Community is infinitely larger than its economic purpose".[6]

Over time the economic purpose seems to have taken on an ever larger role. This can be overstated. At the time of the debates over a European Constitutional treaty and, later, the Lisbon treaty, there was certainly much discussed that was not economic. Much was made of the need to state the case for subsidiarity, the Charter of Fundamental Rights,[7] and of concern for "social Europe".[8]

For all that, the response to the Eurocrisis (a process which has now been with us for some seven years and counting) has revealed that these social issues take a subordinate role to economic performance, and particularly a concern to reduce levels of sovereign debt as quickly as possible, apparently regardless of any social costs. This was made clear by German Chancellor Angela Merkel in 2012 when she stated that "it's our obligation today to do what has been neglected, to break the vicious circle of generating ever more debt and breaking the rules," and that Germany was "convinced that Europe is our destiny and our future. If the Euro fails, Europe fails."[9]

The general point is clear enough – in order to save Europe the answer, according to the Eurozone's most powerful leader, is to break the issue of sovereign debt. In that vein of thinking, there have been repeated enforcements of austerity programmes that have drastically cut welfare states. Some of these austerity rules, most notably of course in Greece, have been imposed centrally by European institutions or leaders and have at times seemed actively and consciously to override democratically legitimate policies and governments in the countries in question.

Certainly in the debates and negotiations over Greece (and indeed other, less extreme, examples), the emphasis from the European institutions and prominent national leaders from creditor nations (notably Merkel) has focused significantly more on debt and reducing national deficits than it has on living and working conditions of European citizens (a critical concern, it might be remembered, of the Treaties of Rome and Paris). The protection of the Euro and a consensus that a reduction of debt is the immediate priority for economic reform in Europe seems to be a problematic fit with the earlier European concern to protect the welfare state and strive to improve the living conditions of citizens (not to mention the lesson of 1953, when half of West Germany's debts were cancelled at the London Debt Accords – a luxury never offered to Greece).

The whole sense of purpose of economics in the European project seems to have switched from a means to an end that would establish solidarity, peace and improved living standards to one in which economic performance is an end in itself – the greatest single priority of the Union. In the preamble to the Treaty of Paris to establish the ECSC, the member states were described as:

> DESIROUS of assisting through the expansion of their basic production in raising the standard of living and in furthering the works of peace; RESOLVED to substitute for historic rivalries a fusion of their essential interests; to establish, by creating an economic community, the foundation of a broad and independent community among peoples long divided by bloody conflicts; and to lay the bases of institutions capable of giving direction to their future common destiny.[10]

That vision seems rather different from what we see today, with the very real prospect of conflict and violence provoked in part by the fact that the EU is seen to be imposing austerity upon its citizens in the face of overwhelming democratic opposition in some states.

Similarly the Treaty of Rome that established the EEC called on "the other peoples of Europe who share their ideal to join in their [member states'] efforts".[11] At that time the European project had a clear belief in its own essential moral purpose and a clear sense that this was an aim to which it wanted to attract other European states. That is quite some transition to today where a member state (Greece) was very nearly forced (as of July 2015, and may yet be forced in the future) to leave the Union because it represented a financial liability.

After decades of efforts at increasing democracy and living standards, suddenly both are being sacrificed to the defence of economic progress.

There is an increasing sense of all other ideals and ends being overridden in today's EU. After decades of efforts at increasing democracy and living standards, suddenly both are being sacrificed to the defence of economic progress for its own sake. It is this that prompted Alexis Tsiparis, even before he became Greek Prime Minister, to criticise the trend and as an emerging "Taliban neoliberalism".[12] Less evocative, but perhaps no less damning, has been the critique of Jurgen Habermas who accuses the EU response to the crisis of being an increasingly "hegemonic technocracy" imposing its economic model in defiance of any democratic legitimacy.[13] This is a European trend which has been increasingly manifesting itself in both European and national government. Slavoj Žižek identifies the same issue in Slovenia in 2012,[14] where a constitutional court ruled that a referendum to establish a "bad bank" in which all toxic debts could be placed and then bought out by government money, should not go ahead (despite having the requisite signatures to be a binding commitment) on the basis that it would have caused "unconstitutional consequences".

The roots of this damaging trend do not begin with the sovereign debt crisis but in a consensus that was allowed to build up from much earlier to the effect that the real reason that Europe matters is that it is beneficial for national *economic* interest. This trend has been summarised by Habermas who argued that

> [I]n its current form the European Union owes its existence to the efforts of political elites who could count on the passive consent of their more or less indifferent populations as long as the peoples could regard the Union as being in their economic interests, all things considered.[15]

This trend is stronger in some member states than in others but has been developing for quite some time. It is in the UK where it has been strongest, however, and it is perhaps no coincidence that it is the UK that is the most likely to leave the EU by its own volition (as opposed to being forced out – per the potential Greek case).

In the UK "Brexit" debate, both sides have drawn up their position primarily on an economic basis. The cases for and against are couched predominantly (though admittedly not exclusively) in terms of which way makes Britain richest. Hence the campaigns of both pro- and anti-EU groups to recruit spokespeople from the financial and business world. The pro side talk about Japanese car-makers threatening to leave the UK if the UK leaves the EU,[16] alongside research that suggests the UK job market relies on the EU.[17] The anti side, meanwhile, argues that the costs of EU regulation and red tape outweigh the benefits[18] and the costs of EU immigration put a severe strain on UK finances.[19] Nigel Farage, the leader of UKIP, is fond of quoting that EU membership costs the UK "£55 million a day".[20]

The debate has become a clash of statistics and contested facts over the respective costs and gains of European membership. Ultimately, however, playing this game hurts the pro-Europe side more than is perhaps recognised. Even if they 'win' the argument – and such arguments rarely have clear winners – they contribute to that consensus that Europe is viable only as a vehicle for improving national economic performance. The scope and ambition of the programme is limited by the extent to which it can demonstrably pay more into treasury coffers than it costs. Ultimately, this is a weak foundation for the European project. Economic performance is variable, as the current crisis shows. As the basis of unity it is hard to sell to a Greek pensioner or a Spanish teenager that the EU has done much to make them richer. Even at its best it would still, ultimately, be a weak *raison d'être*.

Loyalty and affection are not inspired by technical calculations that demonstrate improved national economic performance. If the EU were only a free trade area that might be sufficient, but for a Union that has always aspired to be something more than that it needs something stronger. If it relies on passive consent owed due to technical calculations, it will be forever vulnerable and at the mercy of global economic trends. In the event of a global economic downturn there will be no basis for support and instead the likely result is one of resentment.

The evidence of that shift, from support to resentment, is already becoming apparent. The academics Sara Hobolt and Olaf Cramme have identified an increasing mistrust across Europe of European institutions (in fact more Europeans now mistrust European institutions than trust them).[21] A large number of citizens in some countries (83% per cent in Greece, 47 per cent in Spain and 34 per cent in Italy) now believe that other EU countries pose a "major threat" to their national economies.[22]

This resentment and fear is understandable. As far back as 2009, when the crash was still in its infancy, the consultants McKinsey and Company highlighted a structural issue at the heart of the Eurozone.[23] Germany, helped by the introduction of the Euro with a lower exchange rate than they had previously experienced and a booming export market, were enjoying an enormous current account surplus accounting for 6.4 per cent of GDP. The Netherlands, Austria and Finland benefitted in a similar way from the Euro. By contrast, Spain, Greece, Italy, and Portugal since joining the Euro have been operating with major current account deficits, with Spain's in 2008 equalling roughly 10 per cent of GDP.

During the boom years this was not especially problematic, but during the crash it amplified the crisis considerably. Foreign capital flow decreased significantly in those deficit countries and their exports became less competitive on the global market. Previously they would likely have depreciated their currency in order to boost exports. Without that option it became much harder to incentivise investment and improve the overall situation. As a result, McKinsey estimated in a later report, of all the benefits gained from the Euro among Eurozone members almost 50 per cent have gone to Germany,[24] while Greece, Spain, Italy, and Portugal might actually be worse off than they would have been under their old currency.

Germany has disproportionately benefitted from the Euro at the expense of its Southern European partners, and yet it is the one enforcing austerity measures and punishing the welfare budgets of those same partners today. It should be of little surprise that mistrust directed at the EU and Germany is on the rise among EU citizens, and that the argument that member states should be in Europe because it benefits them economically is struggling to hold up. Despite that, there is little evidence of much progress to present an alternative model. Perhaps this is because the European project has come to forget that it already had an alternative basis in morality.

the loss of the moral and spiritual basis

From the European project's origins, there were three areas that seemed particularly to embody a moral basis for Europe: peace; solidarity and rights; and living standards (especially of workers). In each of these areas there has been a weakening of these moral bases. It is worth looking at each in turn to see the way in which that change has occurred, in addition to looking at one additional moral issue that was not present in the 1950s – the environment – but which is the great, if partial, success story of the moral cause of Europe.

peace

In the section above on the changing context of Europe, it was noted that peace as an aim does not seem to resonate as it once did. In 2011, a Eurobarometer poll found that only 4 per cent of Europeans considered war or civil war to be the most important challenge to national security.[25] It is possible that since 2011 that dimension has changed – not least in the Baltic states and among other Eastern members nervously watching Russian aggression in Ukraine. That itself, though, raises an interesting problem for the EU as an organisation aimed at promoting peace. Three times in the last 25 years Europe has had the opportunity to take a lead on preventing conflict – first the Bosnian war in 1992-5, then the Kosovan war in 1998-9 and, most recently, the Ukraine crisis. Those were three opportunities for the EU to be a global champion for peace in its own region, and represent (by and large) three failures to do so.

In Bosnia, the EC (European Community – the EU not coming into force until the Maastricht treaty, signed in 1994) singularly failed to prevent disintegration and genocide. Malcolm

Rifkind, the then British Defence Secretary, was adamant that military intervention or arming the Muslim Bosnians would prolong or worsen the conflict. This was fiercely opposed by Margaret Thatcher (to the embarrassment of the Prime Minister, John Major) who described the response, correctly with hindsight, as "a little like an accomplice to massacre."[26] Despite Thatcher's criticism, the overall European response (and indeed the UN response) followed Rifkind's route.

The Kosovo war was in many ways a repeat performance. The EU was unable to deliver a co-ordinated response and looked on while NATO performed the role of European intervention force – to the great frustration of British Prime Minister Tony Blair. It did perform an admirable role in negotiations, with the EU envoy Martti Ahtisaari receiving praise for work bringing together an acceptable agreement in ending the war.[27]

There was some hope, after Kosovo, of an expanded and enhanced diplomatic and defence capacity within Europe. Sixteen years later, however, we find the EU has once again proved impotent in preventing a European conflict, with Russia successfully annexing Crimea and continuing to occupy and contest Ukrainian territory. Not only has the EU failed adequately to resolve the conflict, but the accusation has come from a number of sources that EU policy actually provoked Russia in the first place.[28]

Naturally hindsight provides a huge advantage in analysing such conflicts. The idea that there are easy solutions to solving the complex mass of competing religious, ethnic, national, and historical clashes that characterises the Balkans is clearly nonsense. Yet, for all that, it is difficult to escape the sense that having been founded with a strong and explicit purpose of pursuing peace, the European project has stalled in pursuing that aim. That France and Germany are reconciled is an astonishing political achievement after centuries of competing for European dominance. The failure to secure peace on the Union's doorstep must, however, be considered a serious problem. The moral mission to create peace has not been as successful in the past 25 years as it was in the 1950s.

The moral mission to create peace has not been as successful in the past 25 years as it was in the 1950s.

Perhaps underpinning this general failure is the basic point that in the 1950s the European project knew what it was and what it was for. It had a clear sense of identity and was therefore able to be a force for peace confident in what it was defending. Today that is less clear. The impotence of the EU to intervene in crises stems in part from a lack of clarity over what it is that it is meant to defend.

solidarity

How successful the European Union continues to be in terms of solidarity depends rather on the policy in question. There is, for example, a European Union Solidarity Fund (EUSF) which was established after the flooding in Central Europe in 2002. This fund is mostly used to support immediate disaster relief within EU member states. Twenty-four of the twenty-eight member states have drawn money from this fund to help with relief from floods, earthquakes, forest fires, storms, and landslides (only Denmark, Belgium, Luxembourg, and the Netherlands have never claimed). The biggest grants saw around €670 million given to Italy after earthquakes in 2012, €494 million again to Italy for earthquakes in 2009, and €440 million to Germany after floods in 2002.[29] This, then, is a relatively successful example of European co-ordinated measures to support member states dealing with natural disasters. In effect, it functions as an insurance system. Member states pay into the fund and are supported by it should they experience a natural disaster.

This is, in fact, symptomatic of the area in which solidarity continues to be relatively successful, the area of political solidarity that functions as a form of short-term necessary mutual support (in other words, much like an insurance system). It is a sense of solidarity which is consciously divorced from any moral demands. Indeed Habermas in his plea for European solidarity stated frankly that "appeals to solidarity [can] by no means rest on a confusion of politics with morality."[30] He later argues "Offering assistance out of solidarity is a political act that does not at all require a form of moral selflessness that would be misplaced in political contexts".[31] The only solidarity called for by Habermas (and one he feels the Union does not embody enough) is one established in a political context of mutuality.

Such a conception of solidarity is quite divorced from that which was used by Christian Democrats in the 1950s. Their model was explicitly moral, tied up in a conception of human dignity and a sense of justice. However, even were we to accept Habermas's vision of solidarity as opposed to that of the Christian Democrats, the European project is still falling short (as Habermas himself would readily agree). This essay has already argued that economic solidarity has broken down with creditor nations extracting a high price from debtors within the Union despite having disproportionately benefitted from the introduction of the Euro. In debates over sovereign debt there has been little talk of solidarity and support (though the Austrian Chancellor did raise the issue on Greece).

Beyond economics, one of the clearest examples of a failure in solidarity is that of asylum and migration. There were moves in early 2015 to improve this area considerably, with proposals brought forward by the European Commission to support Greece and Italy (the two states most under pressure from migrants and asylum seekers coming by boat from

Syria and North Africa) by relocating some 40,000 migrants to other EU states, resettling 20,000 migrants from outside the EU, taking more co-ordinated action against people smuggling, and developing a new operational plan for military, naval and air assets in the Mediterranean.[32] Those policies, and especially the relocation quotas for migrants, were immediately rejected by the UK, France and the so-called V4 (Visegrad countries – Hungary, Poland, Slovakia and the Czech Republic, each of whom operate extremely tough immigration and asylum criteria). Without co-ordination and consensus there is simply no way that a proper way forward can be found on this issue. Ultimately this could prove to be short-sighted by the opponents. Italy and Greece may decide that rather than take the brunt of costs for policing, housing and processing these people, they might simply wave them through, and without internal European borders that would present both a security risk and a burden placed on other member states to pick up the slack with or without an agreement. Indeed early reports from the November 2015 Paris attacks suggest that this may have already happened, with one of the attackers supposedly having been allowed into the EU via Greece.

Solidarity is talked about a lot in European debates. Indeed, even in the midst of rejecting the packages for migrants and asylum seekers, the joint statement by the V4 read, "While expressing solidarity to member states mostly exposed to migratory pressures, we underline the responsibility of frontline member states to fully implement mechanisms currently in place."[33]

That is quite simply a statement that we believe in solidarity, but we are not prepared to pick up the cost of this issue. This is the situation in which the European project now finds itself: constantly discussing solidarity, and proposing and executing policy that remains determined principally, if not entirely, by short-sighted, individual national interest. The claims made in European treaties are all too rarely carried out in practice and policy.

rights and working conditions

Perhaps no priority of the early European project has found itself so comprehensively undermined as that of working and living conditions of workers. In the 1950s, this was an explicit aim of the European project, operating in tandem with the emergence of welfare states among the original six members.

Compare that with the situation today in which, even before the financial crash and resulting austerity measures, academics were speculating that the EU was itself one of the primary causes of strain on welfare states.[34] The free movement of people, once viewed as an essential tenet of a united Europe and a means of creating a more vibrant economy, is now increasingly viewed by wealthy countries as little more than a licence for "benefit tourism"[35] and a corresponding pressure on welfare services.

> Rights experienced something of a golden age in the 2000s.

Of course, with austerity these pressures have become far more acute, with an extraordinary scaling down of welfare provision in a number of states (most prominently, of course, in the so-called "PIGS" – Portugal, Italy, Greece and Spain). More broadly, the concern for securing better living and working conditions for European citizens now seems firmly established as, at best, a secondary concern.

Rights, on the other hand, experienced something of a golden age in the 2000s. The Lisbon Treaty[36] introduced as a binding treaty commitment the EU Charter of Fundamental Rights. This document contains 54 Articles that include the explicit commitment, among other things, to life, the prohibition of torture, freedom of thought, conscience and religion, academic freedom, and education.

This does include a whole section on the rights of workers including collective bargaining, the right to protection in the event of unjustified dismissal, fair working conditions, and a prohibition on child labour – all of which helps support workers' rights and makes them an act of law. There is, however, even in this something of a shift. The early European treaties did not use rights as their tool of choice. The focus was on collectively improving working conditions and the prosperity of citizens. With the fundamental charter comes a new sense – taking collective purpose and replacing it with what is innately due to the individual. Where once better working conditions was the aspiration of the project as a whole, now they are a legally established minimum duty – and one that, as we have seen, can be readily undermined when the accompanying welfare state and government investment in the economy is heavily cut back.

There is also a wider concern with the use of rights legislation as brought in by European institutions without much by way of democratic oversight. Increasingly it seems like rights are the tool employed by European institutions as the means of building collective responsibility or community. This is part of the technocratic takeover of Europe that so concerns Habermas.[37] The fear is that the use of rights legislation is little more than a means of imposing laws onto citizens without a requisite democratic means to challenge that and engage in will-formation.

Still, for all the associated problems, we can at least see in the development of fundamental rights a legitimate framework for establishing some moral principles. In this regard, if nothing else, the European project continues to exhibit some basis in morality and as a flagship for moral leadership.

the environment

The issue of the environment might also have appeared under either the heading of solidarity or subsidiarity since it certainly is an important feature of both those debates. In terms of solidarity it is clearly an issue that has an impact on all EU citizens and in terms of subsidiarity it is a classic example of a problem which is best met by a co-ordinated Europe-wide response. The reason for separating it from the points above is simply because it is such a large policy area that has consequences for both subsidiarity and solidarity that it merits a section of its own.

The environment is one area in which there has been legitimate and serious progress made at the European level. It was not, of course, a concern in the 1950s, but it is an area in which the EU has come to deliver a series of internationally-led agreements and policies that are among the most ambitious and effective worldwide.

The centre piece of the current system is the EU ETS (European Union Emissions Trading System), the first major and still the largest international greenhouse gas emission trading scheme, launched in 2005. Essentially each member state is given a carbon emissions limit on which basis they allocate allowances to their own industries. Individual industries that struggle to limit themselves to their allowances can increase their limits by trading with other companies who are under the cap. The theory is that businesses are therefore incentivised to cut emissions so that they don't have to buy more allowance from competitors or, better still, so that they can sell emissions quotas themselves.

Overall, the EU ETS forms the critical tool in reaching an EU economy-wide target of a 20 per cent reduction in emissions over the period 1990-2020 and an aspirational 80-95 per cent reduction by 2050. These are, by global standards, ambitious targets and the mechanism to realise them is an innovative one, albeit not without problems. Notably, since 2008 and the financial crisis, the cost of allowances (EUAs) sold to firms reduced from €30 to €4.50 (though this had recovered somewhat to €7.67 by July 2015). Of course, the scheme has been partially successful even with the price decrease because the caps have reduced the amount of carbon produced. However, the reduction in price means that the cost of failure is no longer as significant, dis-incentivising companies to work harder to decrease their emissions by investing in new technology – as the scheme originally envisaged.[38]

There is a fundamentally moral component to these environmental policies. The issue of "climate justice", the idea that environmental change has a disproportionately deleterious effect on those who disproportionately have the smallest environmental footprint, has been gaining momentum in academia in recent years. It is a phenomenon that was beautifully identified in Jonathan Schell's famous 1982 book *The Fate of the*

Earth: "Formerly, the future was simply given to us; now it must be achieved. We must become the agriculturalists of time." Schell was talking about the prospect of nuclear war rather than climate change, but the same sense is present for both crises: saving the future and the Earth has become an active concern of mankind. It is a process that needs to be actively tended and grown. The EU has become a global leader in addressing this particular moral concern.

The environment thus remains the great partial success story of Europe's moral basis – 'partial' because, alongside the success stories there have been failures, both to win consensus and to be ambitious enough in the face of the scale of the task. Current projections predict that a number of EU states will fail to meet its targets, despite the agreements. This is all the more problematic when the target to cut emissions by 40 per cent by 2030 was criticised by Professor Jim Skea, a vice-chair of the UN Intergovernmental Panel on Climate Change, as too weak to meet the necessary task.[39] Future negotiations seem to have become increasingly fraught, especially during the economic crisis. There is hope here, and indeed some effort at conscious moral leadership, but much more to be done.

conclusion

It is not surprising that the European project has changed, both in its specific institutions and its broader ideological output during its 65 or so year history. What is perhaps more surprising is that the fundamental character of the project seems to have changed. What once was a consciously moral, indeed spiritual, project with a number of explicit moral aims and values has come to be predominantly characterised by a particular economic model. Europe has lost its soul – its real sense of both what it essentially is and *why* it exists.

However, all is not lost – there are still reasons to be hopeful that the moral basis of Europe can be rekindled. The sense of solidarity may have dwindled, but in the EU Solidarity Fund and in some proposals both economic and on migration there are still the makings of something greater. Peace may be losing its resonance, and may have failed in Bosnia, Kosovo, and Ukraine – yet there is still the memory of the reunification of Western Europe and an ambition if not yet the power to expand the diplomatic and defence capacities of the EU. In the Charter of Fundamental Rights, Europe has shown there is still a real commitment to something moral, and in its environmental policies there is already a strong base on which to build. The moral basis of Europe has declined since the 1950s but there might yet be a chance to restore it. It is to that hope that the final part of this report turns.

chapter two – references

1. Foreign Secretary Ernest Bevin in October 1950 wrote a memorandum stating that traditional British policy was opposed to the creation of any international blocs – but that the presence of the emerging power of the USSR in Eastern Europe and the state of overall morale in Europe outweighed those concerns. Eurobarometer polls accessible online http://ec.europa.eu/public_opinion/archives/ebs/ebs_371_en.pdf
2. Article 9 E establishes the High Representative of the Union for Foreign Affairs and Security Policy and Article 13 A concerns the European External Action Service.
3. These international networks of inter-war Christian Democrat politicians were critical to the developing ideology of Christian Democracy that came to dominate the Post War period in Western Europe.
4. Srecko Horvat, 'Why the EU needs Croatia more than Croatia needs the EU' in Žižek and Horvat *What Does Europe Want? The Union and its Discontents*, (Istros Books, 2013).
5. The official press release from The International Criminal Tribunal for the former Yugoslavia (ITCY) who conducted the trial can be found online at http://www.icty.org/sid/11145
6. From a speech delivered in the Bundestag as Chancellor of the Federal Republic of Germany, 12 July 1952.
7. The EU charter of fundamental rights became law with the Lisbon Treaty in 2009 and looks at a number of different rights for EU citizens.
8. An explicit concern that was looked at by the European Convention that debated and drafted the aborted Constitutional Treaty, much of which was later adopted in the Lisbon Treaty.
9. Speech delivered in the Bundestag outlining the line Germany would take at a G20 meeting, 14 June 2012.
10. Preamble, Treaty of Paris, 1951.
11. Preamble, Treaty of Rome, 1958.
12. From a preface written for Žižek and Horvat, *What Does Europe Want?* (2013).
13. Jürgen Habermas, *The Lure of Technocracy* trans. Ciaran Cronin (Polity, 2015).
14. 'When the blind are leading the blind, democracy is the victim' from Žižek and Horvat, *What Does Europe Want?* (2013).
15. 'The Lure of Technocracy: A Plea for European Solidarity' in Habermas, *The Lure of Technocracy* (2015).
16. 'Tory anger as Nissan boss warns of leaving UK if we quit EU despite praising firm's 'blessed' Sunderland factory', *Daily Mail*, 9 November 2013.
17. 'UK jobs supported by exports to the EU' a CEBR analysis piece from March 2014 accessible online at http://www.cebr.com/wp-content/uploads/2014/03/UK-jobs-dependent-on-exports-to-the-EU.pdf
18. E.g. 'EU Regulation Costs UK £27.4 Billion A Year – Report', *Huffington Post*, 21 November 2013.

19. 'Revealed: the migrants who costs us £8m EACH DAY' *Daily Express*, 21 April 2015.
20. He has made the claim on a number of occasions but perhaps most prominently during the LBC Leaders Debate on 27 March 2014.
21. Olaf Cramme and Sara B Hobolt, 'A European Union under Stress' in Cramme and Hobolt (eds), *Democratic Politics in a European Union under Stress* (OUP, 2015), p. 3.
22. Sara B Hobolt, 'Public Attitudes Towards the Euro Crisis' in ibid p. 48.
23. Summarised in an article that appeared in *Business Week* 'Imbalances That Strain the Euro Zone', 18 November 2009.
24. McKinsey & Co. 'The Future of the Euro: An Economic Perspective on the Eurozone Crisis' Germany 2012.
25. Eurobarometer poll available online http://ec.europa.eu/public_opinion/archives/ebs/ebs_371_en.pdf
26. Said in a BBC interview, 13 April 1993.
27. See for example p. 3 'European defence post-Kosovo' by Charles Grant, a working paper by the CER (Centre for European Reform), June 1999.
28. Seamus Milne, 'It's not Russia that's pushed Ukraine to the brink of war', *The Guardian*, 30 April 2014.
29. All grants are recorded on the EUSF website – http://ec.europa.eu/regional_policy/en/funding/solidarity-fund/
30. *The Lure of Technocracy*, p. 20.
31. Ibid p. 21.
32. Press released by the Commission on 27 May 2015 – http://europa.eu/rapid/press-release_IP-15-5039_en.htm
33. Quoted in EU Observer https://euobserver.com/beyond-brussels/129256.
34. M. Panić, 'The Euro and the welfare state' in M. Dougan and E. Spaventa (eds), *Social Welfare and EU law* (Oxford: Hart, 2005).
35. 'Economically inactive EU citizens who go to another Member State solely in order to obtain social assistance may be excluded from certain social benefits' Press release of decision by the Court of Justice of the European Union 11 November 2014.
36. The Lisbon Treaty entered into force in 2009 after being agreed in 2007, and largely contains the content of the aborted Constitutional Treaty that was signed in 2004 but rejected in national referenda and abandoned in 2005.
37. *The Lure of Technocracy*.
38. See 'System Responsiveness and the EU ETS' A Dahrendorf Symposium paper from 2013 by Sascha Kollenberg and Luca Taschini.
39. 'Europe emission targets 'will fail to protect climate'' 20 October 2014 http://www.bbc.co.uk/news/science-environment-29690507

3

putting a soul (back) in the union

The European project has reached a point of existential crisis. It began with a clear agenda embedded in the broader politics of post-war Christian Democracy. The immediate need was self-evident – a continent torn apart by war, beset by economic crisis and with an emerging Soviet threat. It also had a clear sense of its own identity, the original six members were all West European, had all just come out of the same conflict and were all largely dominated by politicians who knew one another and shared a common political ideology and religious faith.

Today Europe as a political project has no single clear agenda. Rather than six states sharing similar recent histories and a shared political programme, the EU is now 28 member states with disparate political traditions and recent histories. Eleven of them are only a generation removed from communist rule (not including half of Germany). Two (Spain and Portugal) are only two generations out of fascist dictatorships, while Cyprus remains divided. None of these vivid memories that define national cultures, however, are shared across the EU. Unlike in the 1950s, there is no unifying memory to bind states and create an urgent need for action. The very identity and purpose of Europe are now a matter of confusion, and the project has for some time been sustained only by the will of political elites without much regard to public enthusiasm, legitimisation or, indeed, interest.

> Today Europe as a political project has no single clear agenda.

It is true that there are threats which might yet provide spurs for action. Russia is an increasing concern to the East, Islamic extremism and the related migrant crisis are pressing to the South and South East, the environment is a universal challenge and, of course, there is an ongoing economic crisis. Yet in all this it is notable, as the academics Sara Hobolt and Olaf Cramme have identified, that there has been a conspicuous lack of a "federalist moment".[1]

A 'federalist moment' is that point at which there is such a unifying experience that it becomes possible to take the radical political action of establishing a federal state with confidence that it conforms to the public will. So, for example, the American constitution, which is generally taken as the archetypal product of such a moment, is the political expression of the unifying experience of having become a new nation, free from its previous master and with an ideology of liberty and hope. The Second World War provided such a moment for the early European project – the unifying horror allowed for a seismic political shift in how European states operated and was underpinned by a popular consensus that war on that scale could not happen again. Europe today does not, despite its various crises, have such a moment. There is no overwhelming popular mandate for any change.[2]

What has been fundamentally lost in the Europe of today is a meaningful identity, an appreciation of what Europe is and what it is for. In its place what has come to dominate, as the previous chapters have argued, is a set of confused priorities of which the strongest has been national economic performance. While obviously it is beneficial for the European Union to make its citizens richer, this is a weak basis for a Union to be founded on.

> If the Union's only defence of its own identity is that it makes people richer it will always be vulnerable.

Economic performance is variable and there will inevitably be times when people will feel the effects of economic downturn. If the Union's only defence of its own identity is that it makes people richer it will always be vulnerable. The European project was always meant to be more than economic. Economic prosperity was properly originally considered only to be a means to an end of improving the lives of citizens and building a peaceful Europe characterised by solidarity. That moral, indeed spiritual, basis for Europe is fundamentally a stronger cause for Union *if*, and it is a big if, the EU can recapture such a basis that resonates with its citizens.

This need to recapture and refine the real basis of the European Union, far more than the structural challenges of the Eurozone, will define the future of the European project. The stakes, in fact, are even higher than that. A flourishing EU could point towards the future of international governance and politics. An EU that cannot recapture any such basis is arguably not worth salvaging.

The focus of this part of the report, then, will first look at the task of creating *Europeans* – the long-term and necessary effort to recapture a sense of identity and moral basis of Europe. Second, it will look at the related aspect of remembering Europe's Christian identity. Following that, it will look at a few concrete achievements that might in the short-to-medium term aid that gradual generation process of changing hearts and minds.

making Europeans

The 19th century statesman Massimo d'Azeglio said in 1861, "we have made Italy, now we must make Italians". The aphorism is often quoted because it gets to the heart of the problem that faces many new states. Politically, legally and economically it is possible to create a state with borders marked wherever it is convenient to do so. Europe in the 19th century proved this repeatedly, seeing, for example, the emergence of Italy and Germany from a collection of disparate little states, and the spread of France to take over Savoy. The end of the European empires demonstrated the legal possibilities further with African and Asian states defined and given independence in a way that often bore little resemblance to the borders of ethnic, linguistic, religious, or clan groups. There are, of course, other older European states with similar (arguably) artificial unity – including the UK with its constituent national members and Spain with its significant Catalan, Basque and Galician regions.

Some of these new states have proved remarkably durable, while often retaining some fierce regional identities. Others, over time, have divided or are facing significant pressures. Eastern Europe since the end of communism is the most obvious example of how rapidly pre-political communities can split off. Anyone born in Belgrade in 1918 would today have lived in the Kingdom of Serbia, the Kingdom of Slovenes, Croats and Serbs, the Kingdom of Yugoslavia, the Socialist Federalist Republic of Yugoslavia, the Republic of Serbia and Montenegro and, finally, the Republic of Serbia. Seven different states in less than 100 years without ever having to leave the city! Serbia is extreme but a look at maps of Central and Eastern Europe from 1900 to 2016 shows just how few regions have *not* switched state allegiance in that period. The point is that the institutional foundations for a political entity can be established without really "creating Italians". Creating popular loyalty is a more difficult task than establishing the necessary political and economic structures.

The EU today has a number of separate institutional structures that manage issues of law, economics and politics across member states. Many of these institutions are imperfect or for one reason or another lack the efficacy of their state equivalents. Most notably, there is a common currency, shared by all but a few EU member states, but awkwardly divorced from any unified fiscal policy or other institutional underpinnings – a failing made manifest during the Eurocrisis. Yet despite the presence of these various institutions that constitute the political entity called the EU, there is not yet a recognisable collective European identity. Eurobarometer polls make this quite clear. Only a minority of EU citizens feel attached to the EU to any significant degree.[3]

The European project has existed in a recognisable form since 1952 but despite more and more institutions and centralised bodies coming into being over the subsequent decades, it has failed to move beyond the technical apparatus to creating loyalty, let alone affection among its citizens. Doing so now will be difficult. Other composite political unions (Britain, France, Germany, and Italy for example) created loyalty only very slowly over many generations and still continue to have major fault lines (as the Scottish referendum in Britain showed). They were brought together by some sort of unifying history and culture, that was built upon usually by the imposition of a common language, cultural markers (sometimes including religion), and by collective action against an external threat.

The EU cannot impose a single language or religion and, at present, has no external threat capable of forging unity. For the EU to be a sustainable political entity with the support of its citizens it needs to find its own way of forging that popular loyalty and identity. In some ways, the difficulty facing the EU lies in not wanting to become a single state. If that were the intention it would be much easier to use the familiar tools of statecraft. As it is, the tension lies in wanting to become a political entity that has a collective identity while not wanting to undermine the national and pre-political identities of the member states. This desire not to undermine national identities and member states identities has led to the EU being only a technocratic and institutional set of advances driven by small political elites without much active effort at building any loyalty from citizens.

The European project has become – perhaps has always been – largely an elite-driven, technocratic project. In Jürgen Habermas's words, "in its current form, the European Union owes its existence to the efforts of political elites who could count on the passive consent of their more or less indifferent populations."[4] That this is a problem has long been recognised at both ends of the political spectrum. The 'democratic deficit' as an issue has been addressed by countless academic books and articles and has also concerned European leaders. The efforts in the Maastricht and Lisbon treaties to improve the democratic situation (by increasing the power of the European parliament and by directly electing MEPs, Members of the European Parliament) were sincere, although they have been undermined during the debt crisis, which has been dominated by the European Council (made up of European heads of government) and particularly by the leadership of the French Presidents and German Chancellor.

What much of the academic discourse seems to miss is that the problem is not simply technical – it is not just that democratic accountability in some roles is imperfect, or that the difficulties in responsiveness and representation have not yet been worked out. The issue is the deeper existential problem that the EU has not successfully created Europeans. There is a missing identity.

The academic Larry Siedentop identifies this as a problem which has come from elites pressing forward too rapidly with their technical solutions and leaving public opinion and accountability behind. In *Democracy in Europe* he argued:

Some European nations continue to speak a 'purer' language of federalism, notably the Germans and the Dutch. But that language no longer carries conviction throughout Europe, where public opinion, dazed by the speed with which monetary union is being imposed, and uncertain about its implications, has a growing sense that the elites of Europe have left public opinion far behind... In their pronouncements the elites of Europe have fallen victims to the tyranny of economic language at the expense of political values such as the dispersal of power and democratic accountability.[5]

If that seemed pressing in 2000 it has surely been brought home all the more by the increasingly desperate efforts to allay the Eurocrisis, not least in Greece, where the national democratic will has simply been ignored. For Siedentop, the weakness of the European system is that there can be no reliable rule of law (or indeed functioning political mechanisms) unless rooted in popular habits and attitudes.[6] The only way that the EU can be sustained is if it rests on these popular habits and attitudes that depend, in turn, on shared beliefs – the moral identity of Europe.[7]

This focus on rebuilding the identity and morality of the European project among citizens is surely correct. Without that popular solidarity the EU will continue to rest only on support deriving from successful national economic performance. Jürgen Habermas's vision for accomplishing that aim (of limiting the EU's more elite technocratic trends and creating a more popular and democratic system – an aim shared with Siedentop) is to use an idea of "constitutional patriotism" (in German, *Verfassungspatriotismus*).

Essentially the idea is that by having a democratic constitution that embodies the norms of a plural, democratic society, the citizens of Europe will be able to develop political support and affection for Europe. In other words, Habermas's solution, despite his dislike of technocracy, is fundamentally technical. It relies on a new legal instrument that Habermas hopes will embody the legal norms and values of Europeans in a manner that mirrors the American constitution (a document which undoubtedly carries popular appeal and legitimately embodies something of what it is to be American).

The flaw in the plan is that Europe's previous attempt at a constitution was rejected in referenda in the Netherlands and France. It failed precisely because it was seen as an elite project that did not reflect the values and identity of European citizens. There is little reason to believe, and plenty of reasons to be sceptical, that things have changed today. The fundamental issue is that Habermas assumes that there already actually are underlying values and norms among European citizens that can be expressed in a constitution. In fact, it has been so long since there was a collective identity and moral mission to Europe there are no readily available values on which to draw. Before a constitution or further political institutions are adopted, we first need to build that collective sense of identity and values. We need what Habermas has rejected – a real emotional and pre-political sense of purpose with which to underpin a European project.

To date the most prominent efforts to create such a movement have tended to come from Europe's far left. Alexis Tsiparis, whose remarkable rise from little-known left wing fringe party leader to the man who became Greek Prime Minister and for a moment seemed like the man who would hold the whole Union to ransom, is typical of that trend. In 2013, he summarised the task for the future of Europe as restoring political and moral values above the economic:

> In the years since 1989, the morality of the economy has fully prevailed over the ethics of politics and democracy... Today our task is to restore the dominance of political and social moral values, as opposed to the logic of profit.[8]

Realpolitik took its toll, however, and Tsiparis ultimately buckled to German and EU demands to accept austerity. He has been re-elected (as of September 2015) but it is unclear what the future holds for his party, Syriza. There is not yet any compelling evidence that a Syriza-style vision can win over the European debate. A solidarity and identity based only in protest and resistance to economic austerity is probably no more sustainable in the long-term than one that is based on economic success. It only functions so long as austerity economics is in place during the crisis, and has no other uniting factors, no deeper sense of identity or morality such as Siedentop calls for.

The process of integration will, necessarily, be a long-term one. It is important to remember that the 60 years of peace enjoyed in Western Europe are a significant departure from the norm of European history. Divisions between peoples and nations run deep and, indeed, national identity is often closely bound precisely in opposition to another European nation. London's most prominent public square and one of its largest railway stations are named after victories over the French (Trafalgar and Waterloo). One of Paris's largest stations is Austerlitz, named for Napoleon's greatest victory, while one of France's most famous symbols, the Arc de Triomphe, is a monument to his campaigns. The list could go on, but the point is simple enough: centuries of opposition and conflict that define national literature, symbolism, and identity are not likely to be forgotten quickly.

Building integration ought to have been made easier by the free movement of people enshrined in the Treaty on the Functioning of the European Union.[9] In theory, the ability to move from state to state for work, education and tourism ought to have built a sense of common identity. In practice, the difficulty with this is that the movement of labour has remained one of extremes. Those that move are either drawn from a small mobile elite of Europeans, often working in the financial or legal sectors, or by a larger group of largely unskilled or low-skilled (and low-paid) workers.

The former group is too small to have much impact on the general population's views of other nations; the latter have a tendency to cause resentment and are perceived as either taking jobs from the poorest sections of society or as being a drain on welfare states. One challenge for fostering integration is simply to find ways of making that large middle section, which falls between the two current migrant groups, come to encounter other Europeans.

It is difficult to propose policies as to how this might be done. There are relatively successful university exchange programmes that might bear fruit in the long-term, though, of course, they are only ever going to affect those who go on to study at university (and, indeed, a tiny minority even of those who actually go on the schemes). Ultimately this is a process that is probably best left to grow organically. In practice, there has been a gradual increase (helped by the internet and social media) in interest in foreign sports leagues and the nature of the Eurocrisis has ironically fostered a greater interest in politics in other European states.[10] These are organic processes which will continue in all likelihood regardless of any policy.

Recognising and respecting that there are 'organic processes' necessary to the future of Europe, does not mean the EU ought to do nothing. Rather it ought to learn from its history and recall the words of the Schuman Declaration that led to the original European Coal and Steel Community: "Europe will not be made all at once, or according to a single plan. It will be built through concrete achievements which first create a *de facto* solidarity."[11] Critically these concrete achievements need to be focused on actively building real loyalty, identity and re-establishing the moral purpose of Europe.

It should be noted that there is a danger in this of mistaking activity for action. Given the difficulties at present faced by the EU in seeming overly centralised and dictatorial, care needs to be taken not simply to advance more and more policies and institutions which would merely increase that perception. Political solutions often tend towards the assumption that something can, and therefore must, be done. In fact, this is a scenario in which the expansion of the EU's economic programme and integration in a number of areas has already exceeded what popular capital and support might have allowed. Such concrete steps as are taken from now must look to build up popular support and identification with the EU, not push such support as currently exists beyond breaking point.

a Christian continent?

The question of how far Europe is a "Christian continent", whatever that exactly means, is to some extent the elephant in the room when it comes to building a sense of European identity. The preamble to the Lisbon Treaty refers to the "cultural, religious and humanist inheritance of Europe".[12] The actual content of that inheritance is left broadly undefined, and debates over that line were fierce. A number of countries (and the Pope) pressed for a more explicit mention of Christianity but were ultimately outnumbered by those who wanted to avoid such a gesture. A counter motion to include explicit mention of Europe's secular inheritance and views was also rejected.

There is clearly some irony in all this that the European project had in its foundations, as the previous part of this essay argued, a very strong sense of its Christian identity and a basis in the politics and beliefs of Christian Democrat politicians. In the 1950s it was not controversial to claim a Christian identity for a European political project, except among some fringe Protestant groups. Indeed, the only real point of controversy was whether the early European project could fairly be considered to be Christian as opposed to more narrowly Catholic in outlook.

Naturally that was easier at a time when far more people went to church and considered themselves to be Christian (most of them Catholics). Today there are fewer Christians and also a very different set of histories on the relationship between Church and State. Most of Eastern and Central Europe has experienced decades of enforced authoritarian secularism and the repression of religious groups, followed by an uneven revival in the 1990s. Several of these states are still working out the place of religion in their post-Communist political state. Poland is a good example: the Church undeniably played a role in the fall of Communism, but what role and political respect it is due today is contested. Spain, like the original six members, is a Catholic majority country but the role of the Church in Franco's regime makes it a contentious piece of identity politics.

Many of today's member states retain a secular constitution. Several (the UK, Denmark, Greece, and Malta) retain an established Church. Others, including Sweden, Spain, and Finland, retain complicated constitutional arrangements between Church and State. Malta is particularly remarkable, Article 2 of its constitution reading:

> (1) The religion of Malta is the Roman Catholic Apostolic Religion. (2) The authorities of the Roman Catholic Apostolic Church have the duty and the right to teach which principles are right and which are wrong. (3) Religious teaching of the Roman Catholic Apostolic Faith shall be provided in all State schools as part of compulsory education.[13]

Making the situation still more complicated, of course, is the increase in numbers of both the non-religious and those of non-Christian faiths. Muslims are thought to make up 7.5 per cent of the French population and almost 15 per cent of the Bulgarian population, for example.[14] In the very long-term, Bosnia-Herzegovina, Kosovo, Albania, or even Turkey might one day provide the EU with its first majority Muslim state.

And yet, despite all this, Europe as a continent remains a Christian space, and that ought to be acknowledged in any attempt to think about and create a European identity. Europe is Christian in that Christianity defines the culture, values, history, legal structure, and sense of self-understanding of the space we call Europe, regardless of whether the inhabitants of that space actually believe in or even affiliate to Christianity. Europe has no other claim to be a continent than this intellectual, cultural space. The Eastern border with Asia (currently considered the Urals) is entirely arbitrary and has been redrawn on a number of occasions. Cyprus is considered European and is an EU member state, despite lying far closer to Lebanon (about 160 miles) than to the nearest mainland European coastline (it is almost 700 miles from Greece). Malta, another EU member, is closer to Tunisia than Italy. European football competitions include Israel, Azerbaijan, Georgia, Kazakhstan, and Turkey, as does the Eurovision song contest, which last year, bizarrely, also included Australia. Europe, to adopt Benedict Anderson's famous phrase, is an "imagined community" – and a crucial part of the content of the imagined bond is Christianity.

It is not, to be sure, defined only by its Christianity but neither is it possible to remove Christianity from the equation. Emmanuel Levinas defined Europe as "the Bible and the Greeks,"[15] to which others might add the Enlightenment or Marxism.[16] This should not by any means be taken to be an exclusivist position. It does not deny the 'European-ness' of those who are not Christians and it certainly doesn't necessitate the resurrection of Christendom or of theocratic governance.

However, it is to argue that a Europe that does not remember what it is and where it has come from is weaker for that failure. To develop a really meaningful identity for Europe (as a successful Union surely must if it is to have real longevity) the Christian element must be remembered.

concrete steps

There are, of course, any number of possible proposals for concrete steps towards rebuilding the moral nature of the European Union. The ones proposed here are not intended to be comprehensive or even to mark the whole breadth of the field. They are also intended only to be steps towards changing the culture of the European Union and popular attitudes as to what Europe is really for. None of these policies is a silver bullet or individually capable of changing the nature of European politics. Yet it is hoped that by the gradual accumulation of these morally-based policies that the Union might slowly recapture its moral identity. To that end, this essay proposes five areas in which concrete steps could be taken, each related to existing policy areas and concerns from the history of the European project: solidarity, subsidiarity, employment and working conditions, peace, and the environment.

solidarity

Solidarity, as this report has argued, has always been a concern of the European project, even if it seems to have become hollowed out over time. It is really the single foundation on which the whole European project rests and is closely tied into exactly the issues of collective identity and morality discussed above. One concrete step that could re-establish the Union's commitment to solidarity and fill a clear moral need for its citizens would be to take firm action to resolve the refugee and migrant crisis.

At the time of writing this is already a process which has, in fairness, received significant EU attention. The Commission President Jean-Claude Juncker used his annual State of the Union address in September 2015 to introduce a new plan for confronting the crisis.[17] This proposes mandatory redistribution quotas so that refugees are spread throughout the member states more evenly, a new fund to address root causes of migration in Africa, and a Europe-wide 'safe countries of origin' list of countries to which failed asylum seekers can be safely returned.

That there are firm proposals is a positive step, but as they stand they are both likely to cause resentment and insufficient to solve the crisis. Compulsory quotas are extremely unpopular with some member states, and though there is now a majority voting system in place that has allowed Juncker's proposal to become official policy, in the face of such opposition it risks seeming like another dictatorial measure from the European centre enforced against the wishes of some members.[18] If compulsory quotas are enforced it could easily undermine solidarity, creating resentment in some member states and a possible backlash against the refugees allocated to those countries.[19] Quotas also miss the problem that there is nothing to stop a refugee moving to another country from the one that they were allocated once they have arrived.

The logic behind the quotas is the recognition that some countries bear the brunt of the current crisis. Not only is that problematic in terms of what is fair to those countries but it also has serious consequences in terms of the asylum seekers' welfare. Currently so overwhelmed are the frontline member states (Greece, Cyprus, Italy, Malta, and Hungary) that they are failing correctly to process or administer the asylum seekers who arrive. As a result, many people with legitimate cases are rejected simply due to administrative burdens.[20] That is morally problematic in itself, but becomes worse when many of those failed asylum seekers then attempt to reach other countries, taking significant risks to their own lives in doing so, and are met by mistrust and resentment when they arrive.

Rather than rely on quotas, however, there are other ways to ease the burden on those frontline countries. First, the appalling dangers braved by asylum seekers on overcrowded and unsafe boats launched without crew from North Africa and the Middle East could be greatly reduced with a better Europe-wide search-and-rescue service in the Mediterranean. In the year following October 2013, an Italian search and rescue service, 'Mare Nostrum', patrolled the Italian and Libyan coasts confronting smugglers and helping refugees. It could not stop all the boats, but it significantly reduced the scale of the problem. When 'Mare Nostrum' became the EU-wide Operation Triton in October 2014 it was a significantly reduced operation that patrolled only European waters, with only a small number of ships and aircraft, no mandate to search and rescue the boats, and a much smaller budget. The results have been disastrous. In the first three months of Triton there was a 160 per cent increase in migrants compared with the same period the year before, and a significant increase in reported deaths in the Mediterranean.[21] A well-funded EU mission in the Mediterranean including more ships and aircraft and a mandate to patrol across the Mediterranean and to perform search-and-rescue missions would reduce the risk of deaths at sea. It would also reduce the number of boatloads of people currently putting such strain on those countries currently over-burdened with asylum seekers.

The process could be improved still further if there were a reform of the current Dublin System[22] that forces asylum seekers to arrive in an EU member state before they can apply for asylum or a visa. What this means in practice is that rather than take the perfectly safe ferry services from North Africa for which a ticket costs less than €50, refugees are instead forced to use smugglers' boats which, apart from being far more dangerous, also cost the refugee anywhere between US$2,000 and US$10,000.[23] A Centre for European Policy Studies policy brief in September 2015 highlighted this issue and called for alternative tools for refugees to arrive safely and legally – including reforms of the visa system.[24]

This situation is not helped by the fact that alongside the Dublin System there is a lack of coherence among national regulations on authorised immigration and visa requirements. Family reunification is a case in point, with substantial national variance on criteria for consideration.[25]

With regard to unauthorised migration, and particularly to address the crisis of refugees and deaths in the Mediterranean, one solution would be to set up safe spaces for refugees outside Europe's borders in North Africa and the Middle East from which asylum and visa applications to different member states could be submitted. This would reduce the dangers and costs of having to cross the Mediterranean, reduce the burden of administration on frontline South European countries, and allow for a better redistribution system among member states at the point of application (rather than after they have already arrived in Cyprus, Italy or Greece).

Adopting such measures as a means of building solidarity has the huge advantage at present that there is a clear public enthusiasm for some sort of action to counteract the humanitarian crisis in the Mediterranean. It is also a problem that demands an EU rather than national response and is, to an extent, a problem for which solutions can be found, if, sadly, not one that may be eradicated.

subsidiarity

It is notable that at both ends of the political spectrum a consistent critique of the EU and particularly its recent efforts to alleviate the financial crisis has been that it is insufficiently democratic and accountable. For the right, the concern is that the EU is too interventionist in national sovereignty and fails to take onto account the wills of national parliaments. For the left, it is the imposition of austerity despite public opinion that causes concern. The 'Democratic Deficit' is an issue that has exercised scholarship in European politics for decades, but shows no sign of going away.

It is not that there have not been efforts to improve democracy and, in the spirit of subsidiarity, bring politics closer to the level of the European citizen. The introduction of the European parliament with directly elected MEPs was an effort in that direction. Successive treaties have increased (at least in theory) the power of the parliament. Jean-Claude Juncker's selection as President of the European Commission, the *de facto* president of the EU, was the first that was meant to involve a degree of democratic oversight rather than simply being selected by national leaders.

However, these measures have stopped well short of being effective. The selection process for the President of the Commission is illustrative of the general problem. The previous system was that national leaders in the European Council came to an informal agreement and then selected their preferred candidate as the President of the Commission. This was a process without transparency and only a very indirect relationship to democratic will. The new system, established in 2013, sees the political parties of the European Parliament propose their own leading candidates for the role (*Spitzenkandidat*). The party that performs best in the European elections will then see their candidate become head of the Commission. For one thing this is absurdly over complicated and not widely understood by the electorate. For another, it is not clearly established in law and has been met with a series of challenges. A third issue is that it seems inherently vulnerable – the election of Juncker was opposed by David Cameron, the British Prime Minister, and it seemed for a period as if the national leaders would simply reject Juncker regardless of the wishes of the parliament.

Most problematically of all, though, is the basic issue that this doesn't seem to make the process any more democratic. The President of the Commission has considerable power to set European policy yet is not directly elected. The largest party in the European parliament is unlikely to control an absolute majority, so it is a moot point whether this understanding ever selects a representative view even of the parliament, never mind the electorate. Public accountability and oversight of the President once selected is extremely limited, not least when the European parliament is itself democratically problematic.

In the UK, only 11 per cent of voters think they can name their MEP (versus 52 per cent who think they can name their national parliament MP).[26] Across Europe, in 2013 half of Europeans could not recall having seen any recent coverage of European Parliament in the media.[27] Accordingly, there is fairly minimal oversight of their work. There is a fundamental problem that institutions can be shown as being democratically responsive to citizens only when they are dealing with issues of public salience and when they have electoral incentives to do so (i.e. politicians do what the public wants only when it's an issue that the public cares about and when they can be punished or rewarded by the public for acting on it).[28] Too much European Union activity lacks real electoral incentives and so doesn't actually respond to democratic will at all.

Accordingly, it is perhaps little surprise that technocratic solutions can be imposed on member states regardless of the popular will in those countries. This is an issue that needs urgently to be addressed. If the President of the Commission is going to be tasked with responding to issues of public concern like financial crises and the refugee crisis, then European citizens ought to be directly electing the man or woman they believe best represents the solutions they want. If the European parliament is to be a true check and balance and set policies then it needs to work harder to be a visible presence in its citizens' lives. If the European project is going to survive then it will need fewer interventions by national leaders to set the overall agenda.

As a minimum, the establishment of a directly elected President of the Commission whose programme and performance would be accountable to European citizens seems sensible. Similarly essential is a clear separation of powers established in the treaty between Council, Commission and Parliament to prevent confusion of roles and unwarranted interference.

employment and working conditions

This report has already argued at some length that a Union based solely on economic performance is inherently vulnerable. However, the economic dimension is important in terms of one key moral demand, which is that from its origins the European project was meant to support and improve working conditions. To an extent this is tied to strong economic performance, which can be harnessed to underpin a strong and effective welfare system and will sustain high levels of employment. Clearly no one would want to propose anything other than good economic performance. The difficulty lies in identifying what the end of such economic performance is, whether reducing debt deficits and improving GDP is an end in itself, or merely a means to supporting employment, working conditions and the dignity of citizens.

The latter was the intention of the early European project – economic gains were made for the sake of workers and citizens. That sense of the ultimate end of economics that underpinned the moral identity of early European integration economics seems to have been lost. Welfare states and employment have been put under significant strain in order to reduce the debt deficit as swiftly as possible. The impact this has on society is significant – and that is increasingly acknowledged (if inadequately resolved) by EU institutions.

László Andor, the European Commissioner for Employment, Social Affairs and Inclusion, is a good example of this increasing awareness of the need to shore up this dimension of European policy. In September 2014, he wrote an article for the EPC (European Policy Centre) which conceded the failure of the EU socio-economic strategy "Europe 2020" that had been agreed in 2010.[29] That strategy had targets for employment and the reduction of poverty based on increasing convergence between different member states. Despite those targets, employment, which was meant to reach 75 per cent EU wide by 2020, has seen a significant drop since 2008, and there has been a significant increase of people in poverty.

Andor goes on to highlight different Commission policies designed to address the issue, but critically holds short of conceding that the policies enforced on some debtor countries (particularly Greece) are likely to seriously undermine the aims and objectives for which he is responsible. If there is to be a way forward that builds the moral identity of Europe, then it must be an economic policy that places the social element of economic policy at the very heart of its mission.

Such a statement is easy to make, but difficult to square with the political realities of managing the chaos of the European financial crisis. Nevertheless, there are ways in which the two can be married more happily than has occurred to date. One example is the future management of Greece and the battles over its debts and budgets. Thus far the most obvious effects of 'solving' the crisis in Greece have been political instability, popular unrest, heavy raids on pensions, appalling levels of unemployment, and a welfare state that looks worryingly under-resourced and overstretched.

There are other ways in which the debt crisis could be managed that would not leave creditors out of pocket but would also allow for a stronger welfare system. One such approach is the possible use of GDP-indexed bonds. One of Greece's biggest difficulties is that without significant income from taxation or investment it spends a disproportionately large part of its budget simply paying off the interest on its loans. The advantage of issuing GDP-indexed bonds is that while the total debt remains, the interest is matched to the state of the country's GDP. In times of poor economic performance interest payments remain relatively low, freeing up more budget space to be spent on welfare policies and significantly reducing the chance of defaulting on a loan.[30] If the economy improves then interest payments increase. This is not a recent or radical economic idea (it has been proposed in the past by both the Bank of England[31] and the IMF[32]) but would serve as an effective measure to preserve budget space for vital welfare services.

peace

It may seem counter-intuitive to propose concrete policies to assuring peace in Europe – after all, it has been 70 years since the end of the Second World War. However, there are a number of clear issues on which a more European approach would be beneficial and build the moral identity of the Union.

It is a serious issue that the European Union is unable to provide a collective military response to issues on its doorstep. The failure in Kosovo ought to have spurred serious progress, but it has not. In the event of a crisis in the Baltic States and Russia, there is no reason to believe that the EU would be in any position to respond before it is too late. The failure to co-ordinate even on something as relatively easy as joint naval operations to stem the crisis in the Mediterranean is extremely worrying.

This does not yet require a fully integrated single EU military (though such a move has been called for by, for example, the historian and international relations expert Brendan Simms[33]). Such a proposition might in the long-term make sound strategic and economic sense to EU member states, but there is little appetite for it in the immediate future. There is space, however, for a looser relationship involving the sharing of information, joint operations and expeditionary forces and efforts to make equipment mutually compatible (e.g. designing ships that will be able to launch the planes and weapons of other EU member states). There is already a model for what such a relationship might look like in the Anglo-French Defence Treaty (the Lancaster House Treaty of 2010), which was extended in 2014.[34] Such co-operation would make sound financial sense given that EU member states have for years now been seeking to economize and reduce their military expenditure[35] and would provide the basis for a defence force better able to respond to crises.

Not only does Europe need better co-ordinated militaries but it also needs to begin to take a bit more responsibility to use those militaries to intervene in issues in its neighbourhood – rather than outsourcing operations to other bodies. The Common Security and Defence Policy (CDSP) is meant to serve as a crisis management response, but in practice has in recent years increasingly relied on outsourcing crisis interventions to other bodies (notably the African Union [AU] and United Nations). The moral cost of this outsourcing is not only that the EU is failing to take the responsibility for action that it claims to want to take, but also that it leaves operations in the hands of less capable forces. Poorly equipped, and with inadequate training, AU operatives are proving unable to perform the necessary task.[36] Accordingly, AU operations have taken significant losses in Somalia and elsewhere, despite EU funding. The failure of the EU to act effectively prolongs conflicts and increases casualties.

Supporting and building peace is not just about the military. The great success of the European project has been to create a political and economic environment in which peace flourishes (since it is more beneficial to a member state for there to be peace than conflict). Underpinning this has been a commitment to human rights and liberal democracy. New candidate states to join the EU need to demonstrate a commitment to democracy and human rights (the "Copenhagen Criteria") before they can be considered as members. Where the situation becomes problematic is what happens if a member state having joined the EU begins to 'backslide' and become more authoritarian or corrupt.[37]

This issue is one of mounting concern particularly in Hungary where the Fidesz party and Victor Orbán were undoubtedly popularly elected, but have introduced a new constitution that critics suggest fundamentally undermines government accountability, human rights and the rule of law.[38] To guarantee the political environment that has underpinned peace so far in Europe, action will need to be taken to determine the legal and political responses needed to protect liberal democracy.

the environment

Environmental policy, the last point in this chapter, is the great partial success story of Europe's moral mission: successful because there have been real efforts (some of them very ambitious by international standards), partial because they have been inconsistent and many have not gone far enough. One concrete step that would build up the EU's environmental policy would be to introduce a more consistently environmentally-committed policy on the import of coal and energy.

At present, the EU imports energy and coal from a number of its neighbours including Serbia, Montenegro, Ukraine and Turkey. Each of these countries uses energy exceedingly inefficiently, with Ukraine consuming 11 times as much energy per unit as the European average.[39] All four are trying to increase their use of coal so as to export more energy to the EU. If the EU is to be a creditable environmental body this cannot be permitted. It damages the environment, creating direct health consequences for EU citizens. It undermines other EU energy policies if neighbouring states are not improving their own performance and it undermines common European security if member states are reliant on foreign imports.[40]

A stronger moral identity, committed to environmental policies, would take action actively to fix this problem by refusing to import energy from those countries that don't reach an adequate efficiency threshold. Not only would this establish a strong moral stance on the issue from the EU but it would also be an action of direct benefit to the health of EU citizens and provide economic advantages for the EU internal market (which would lose a competitor with lower prices due to lower environmental standards).

conclusion

Putting the soul back in the Union by rediscovering its sense of its own identity and moral mission will not be a swift process. It may, in fact, be simply impossible. Europe is not what it was in the 1950s, and the 28 member states may simply be too far apart ever to get back to the cohesive sense of identity and morality that the early European project once had.

If it is to be successful then, there needs to be a gradual shift among Europe's citizens. There must be a popular will to identify something in Europe that is moral and resonates with their own sense of identity. Such a sense is impossible to manufacture overnight – not least when the EU, by detaching itself from citizens and abandoning much of its moral cause, has made the task much more difficult than it would once have been.

However, the EU is not totally impotent in the process of building up its sense of identity and moral mission. There are concrete steps deliberately targeted at areas of moral importance and public salience that might gradually help in the process. There may yet be a chance to save the soul of the Union.

chapter three – references

1. Olaf Cramme and Sara B Hobolt (eds.), *Democratic Politics in a European Union Under Stress* (OUP, 2015), p. 11.
2. A 2012 YouGov-Cambridge poll is typical of general trends, using data from seven EU member states (UK, France, Germany, Italy, Norway, Sweden and Denmark) it found that none of the countries had more than 29 per cent strongly in support of the idea of a United States of Europe (in Denmark, Sweden and the UK it was less than 5 per cent), and only Italy had a majority who tended to be supportive of the idea.
3. 46 per cent feel attached to the EU versus 52 per cent feeling no attachment (compared to 91 per cent who felt attached to their country) according to the Standard Eurobarometer 77, Spring 2012.
4. Jürgen Habermas, *The Lure of Technocracy*, tr. Ciaran Cronin, (Polity, 2015), p. 3.
5. Larry Siedentop, *Democracy in Europe*, (Allen Lane, the Penguin Press, 2000), p. 124-5.
6. Ibid, p. 225.
7. Ibid, p. 189.
8. Foreword to Slavoj Zizek and Srecko Horvat *'What Does Europe Want?' The Union and its Discontents*, (Istros books, 2013), p. 14.
9. Amended and incorporated into the Lisbon Treaty effective as of 2009 and available online http://eur-lex.europa.eu/legal-content/EN/TXT/?uri=CELEX:12007L/TXT
10. Among many other papers see Maurits Meijers 'The Euro-crisis as a catalyst of the Europeanization of public spheres? A crosstemporal study of the Netherlands and Germany' LEQS Paper No. 62/2013 June 2013.
11. The Schuman Declaration is available online - http://europa.eu/about-eu/basic-information/symbols/europe-day/schuman-declaration/index_en.htm
12. The Preamble to the Lisbon Treaty is available online - http://eur-lex.europa.eu/legal-content/EN/TXT/?uri=CELEX:12007L/TXT
13. The Maltese Constitution is available online http://justiceservices.gov.mt/DownloadDocument.aspx?app=lom&itemid=8566
14. Data drawn from Pew Centre's Global Religious Futures project - http://www.globalreligiousfutures.org/explorer/custom#/?subtopic=15&chartType=map&data_type=percentage&year=2010&religious_affiliation=23&age_group=all&pdfMode=false&regions=Europe
15. Levinas, "The Bible and the Greeks" in *In the Time of the Nations* (1986).
16. See Glendinning 'Derrida's Europe: 'Greek, Christian and Beyond" in Agnes Czajka and Bora Isyar (eds), *Europe After Derrida: Crisis and Potentiality*, (Edinburgh University Press, 2014).
17. See Press Release 'Refugee Crisis: European Commission takes decisive action', 9 September 2015.

18 Analysts at the Open Europe think tank believed that, in fact, opposition was sufficient that even using a majority vote system this policy would still have failed. See 'Mandatory redistribution quotas still off the table as EU grapples with refugee crisis' by Nina Schick on the Open Europe blog - http://openeurope.org.uk/blog/mandatory-redistribution-quotas-still-off-the-table-as-eu-grapples-with-refugee-crisis/ In fact the measures passed as of the 23 September 2015, but caused a bitter row – summarised in *The Times* as 'Migrant quotas drive a wedge through Europe' 23 September 2015.

19 This warning was echoed in the CEPS policy brief 'The 2015 Refugee Crisis in the European Union' by Guild, Costello, Garlick and Moreno-Lax, No.332, September 2015.

20 This issue was highlighted by Mortera-Martinex and Koteweg in a blog for the Centre for European Reform (CER) 'Dead in the water: Fixing the EU's failed approach to Mediterranean migrants' April 2015.

21 Reported by Frontex, the European Agency for the Management of Operational Cooperationat the External Borders of the Member States of the European Union, in their quarterly report October-December 2014.

22 The Dublin System includes the Dublin Regulation which is the law governing EU member states' responsibilities on asylum and EURODAC regulation that established an EU-wide database of fingerprints of unauthorised migrants.

23 Statistic on what people pay to get to Europe drawn from UN Office on Drugs and Crime.

24 'The 2015 Refugee Crisis in the European Union' Guild, Costello, Garlick and Moreno-Lax, no.332, September 2015.

25 See 'Common EU policies on authorised immigration: past present and future' Georgia Mavrodi, LSE Ideas Strategic Update 15.2, May 2015.

26 Reported in *The Guardian*, 'Voters can't name their MEPs as poll highlights disengagement with EU' 10 May 2014 http://www.theguardian.com/politics/2014/may/10/voters-cant-name-their-mep

27 Reported in a December 2013 Eurobarometer poll available online: http://www.europarl.europa.eu/pdf/eurobarometre/2013/election3/SyntheseEB795ParlemetreEN.pdf)

28 See 'Democratic Responsiveness in the European Union: the Case of the Council' LEQS Paper No.94/2015 Christopher Wratil, June 2015.

29 László Andor 'Social Europe. Can the EU again improve people's life prospects?' in *Challenge Europe* Issue, 22, September 2014.

30 These advantages were noted in Bank of England Working Paper no. 484 'GDP-linked bonds and sovereign default' by Barr, Bush and Pienkowski in January 2014. This paper is available online http://www.bankofengland.co.uk/research/Documents/workingpapers/2014/wp484.pdf

31 Ibid.

32 As far back as September 2002 there was an IMF Policy Discussion Paper by Borensztein and Mauro 'Reviving the Case for GDP-Indexed Bonds' available online: https://www.imf.org/external/pubs/ft/pdp/2002/pdp10.pdf

33 See, for example, Brendan Simms 'We eurozoners must create a United State of Europe' *The Guardian* 23 April 2013 http://www.theguardian.com/commentisfree/2013/apr/23/united-state-of-europe-anglo-american-union

34 See Press Release 'UK and France agree closer defence co-operation' 31 January 2014 https://www.gov.uk/government/news/uk-and-france-agree-closer-defence-co-operation

35 See John C. Stevens 'Some remarks on the Anglo-French defence treaty', LSE IDEAS Strategic Update 11. 4 November 2011, p. 4.

36 Summarised in Richard Gowan and Nick Witney's ECFR Policy Brief 'Why Europe Must Stop Outsourcing its Security', December 2014.

37 See for example the report by the think tank Demos 'Democracy in Europe can no longer be taken for granted...' by Birdwell, Feve, Tryhorn, and Vibla, 2013 available online - http://www.demos.co.uk/files/DEMOS_Backsliders_report_web_version.pdf

38 See, for example, Bojan Bugarič 'Protecting Democracy and the Rule of Law in the European Union: The Hungarian Challenge' 2015.

39 Stephen Tindale and Suzanna Hinson 'Cleaning the neighbourhood: How the EU can scrub out bad energy policy' a report by the Centre for European Reform, April 2015, p. 3.

40 Ibid.